HEART ZONES CYCLING

Boulder, Colorado

HEART ZONES CYCLING

The Avid Cyclist's Guide to
Riding Faster and Farther

SALLY EDWARDS
SALLY REED

DISCLAIMER

Before starting any exercise program, it's important to have a complete physical examination. Men over age forty and women over age fifty should have a medical examination and diagnostic exercise test before starting a vigorous exercise program, as should symptomatic men and women of any age. If in doubt, consult your physician for clearance.

Intellectual Property Rights/Trademarks: Heart Zones, Heart Zones Training, and other Heart Zones USA brand trademarks and names are registered or unregistered trademarks of Heart Zones USA. All rights are reserved.

All written materials including text, graphs, charts, images, templates, and designs are the property of Heart Zones USA. All rights are reserved.

For permission to use Heart Zones USA trade name, trademarks, and copyrights, please send a written request to:

Heart Zones USA Property Rights
2636 Fulton Avenue #100
Sacramento, CA 95821
USA

VeloPress®, a division of Inside Communications, Inc.
1830 North 55th Street
Boulder, Colorado 80301–2700 USA
303/440-0601; fax 303/444-6788; e-mail velopress@insideinc.com

To purchase additional copies of this book or other VeloPress books, call 800/234-8356 or visit us at www.velopress.com.

Distributed in the United States and Canada by Publishers Group West

Cover design by Stephanie Goralnick
Cover photo courtesy of Getty Images; back cover photo by Chris Milliman; illustrations by Ed Jenne
Interior design and composition by Brent Wilcox

Library of Congress Cataloging-in-Publication Data
Edwards, Sally, 1947-
   Heart zones cycling : the avid cyclist's guide to riding faster and farther / Sally Edwards and Sally Reed.
      p.   cm.
   Includes bibliographical references and index.
   ISBN-13: 978-1-931382-84-7 (pbk. : alk. paper)
   1. Cycling—Training.   I. Reed, Sally, 1948-   II. Title.
   GV1041.E39 2006
   796.6—dc22

                                                                    2006010197

Printed in the United States of America
10 9 8 7 6 5 4 3 2

CONTENTS

FOREWORD

You would think that training for cycling would be easy. Sure, you might get sore from spending so much time in the saddle and your knees could feel creaky now and then, but when it comes to training you just get on the bike and ride, right?

If you have done even minimal reading on how to get results in cycling, you know that a lot of people who write about training seem to be part of a grand conspiracy to make training difficult. If you've ever looked for a personal coach, then you have absolute proof of this conspiracy. Maybe you've even gone to an exercise physiologist—surely they ought to know how to get training right. Sadly, you probably left confused yet again. Perhaps Lance Armstrong deserves a PhD because he obviously knew enough about training to win the Tour de France seven times! You would think that someone could make this stuff simple for the rest of us.

Well, Sally Edwards and Sally Reed have done it. In *Heart Zones Cycling*, you'll find useful information that is simple, practical, and understandable. The proven Heart Zones Training approach begins with the essence of why you are on the bike in the first place (your goals) and progresses to concepts that are typically difficult (thresholds, target heart rate, and power). Edwards and Reed even give you rides that can be modified to suit your training at different times of the year. It's not a cookbook. You still have to make your own decisions and you still have to push the pedals, but *Heart Zones Cycling* will demystify training and help you sort through the confusion about different ways to train.

I've known Sally Edwards for nearly twenty years as an athlete, teacher, businesswoman, and author. In addition to having an MS in exercise physiology from UC Berkeley, she is a former elite Ironman competitor, the author of *The Heart Rate Monitor Book for Cyclists* (a book that opened everyone's eyes to the possibility of using heart rate monitors to optimize training and racing), and quite possibly the person who coined the phrase "crosstraining." I had an argument with Sally within the first five minutes of meeting her. That's Sally's way, always trying to cut through the BS thrown out by the science types. And, that argument was just the first of many. But in the process of arguing with Sally I've become a better scientist, and I like to think that she has become better in her role as one of the primary translators of fitness.

Whether you are a serious competitive cyclist, a dedicated century T-shirt collector, or just using your bike to keep middle age at bay, this book will provide you with a simple, no-nonsense approach to the sport that incorporates the best scientific data with the best training methodology, bar none.

Carl Foster, PhD
Professor of Exercise and Sport Science
University of Wisconsin–La Crosse

PREFACE

With all the training books out on the market, you may be wondering what makes this book different and what compelled us to write it. First, what sets this book apart from most other books about training and cycling is that we do not just give you a prescribed plan and a bunch of great rides and tell you to do what we say. That is not the Heart Zones way. We want you to understand why you are riding the rides you are riding and how to adjust your training program to fit your individual needs. Unlike some other cycling coaches who keep their methodologies pretty close to the vest, we want to share with you the reasoning behind our methodology and empower you to design the training program that works best for you and your goals.

Are you ready for a new way of riding? Want to start seeing better results than you have been getting in the past? Read the following statements—they will get you thinking about the reasons you ride; they also speak to the reasons we wrote this book. How many of these statements do you agree with?

- I would like to get the positive results of training using heart rate technology.
- I would like to update my cycling using the new "universal training language."
- I would consider using the new technologies that measure power, oxygen, and metabolism.

- I would like to do rides that have specific training focus and that fit into a training system individualized for me.
- I would like to create training zones.
- I am confused about "periodization" and would like to understand it better.
- I am looking for sample training plans that are periodized.
- I am ready to coach myself (paraphrasing an old parable, I am ready to "learn how to fish" rather than be given someone else's fish).
- I would like to have a clear understanding of threshold and how to use this crossover point in my training.
- I want to learn how to set goals that I can actually attain.
- I have wondered why training has worked for my riding partners but not for me.
- I suspect that there is no single "one way" to ride, but rather a combination of different training methods that might work best for me.

We feel certain that you agreed with almost all of those statements, just as we did when we began to systematically apply the Heart Zones methodology to our own cycling training twenty years ago. We know there is a better way to ride; there is a training system that works best for your physiology and the type of rider that you are, with your heart, your emotions, and your metabolism.

You are about to learn the latest in cycling training so you can boost your performance, but even more, you are about to connect with new riding tools that will take your riding to the next level and raise your performance bar. Read on. We are with you all the way.

Sally Edwards
CEO, Heart Zones

Sally Reed
Heart Zones Cycling
Chief Developer

ACKNOWLEDGMENTS

Our cycling, professional, and writing careers have been touched by many people. We can never thank enough of our friends and family who have supported each of our individual pursuits and paths along the way. As we bring together our knowledge, years of experience, and thousands of hours on the bike, we again realize none of this would be possible without "Our Team," the people who are always there in body and spirit, cheering us on. A special thanks to those who have so generously provided us with special retreats to "foxhole" where we could write this book: Jeff and Anne Holden for the "cabana and fringe benefits"; John Taylor for the "Vashon with a View" cabin and great island cycling; Suzanne Strom-Reed for the "Wireless Whidbey Cottage" and, yes, more great cycling; and to our new friends in the town of Markleeville, and the ever challenging mountain passes that draw us to them.

YOU,
THE RIDER

1

Define your
goals

Determine your
anchor heart
rate

Set your heart
zones

Periodize your
training load

Design your
training plan

Log your rides

Assess and
adjust

With Heart Zones Cycling, riding is all about you, the rider. As you read each of the next nine chapters, you are going to learn a whole new way of training. To appreciate this new way of training, think for a moment about the old way: In the old way of riding, you may have paid more attention to the *ride* than to *you*. In the old way, you may have recruited riding partners and followed a ride plan that did not fit your training needs. In the old way, you may not have looked at your personal framework and matched your unique needs to your training program. In the old way, you may not have measured your metabolic health to determine its capacity for exercise stress. In the old way, you may not have assessed your current emotional stress to see how it impacts your riding performance. In the old way, you may not have known that there is a new way to ride that leads to riding your best.

Heart Zones Cycling is the new way. It makes you a better rider because it is personalized for you—for the unique individual that you are. It takes its cues from your heart, your physiology, and your unique responses to everything that affects your riding. Whether you are relatively new to the sport or have been a competitive cyclist for a long time, Heart Zones Cycling gives you a new way to ride—a new way to better fitness, faster times, longer distances, and more enjoyment on the bike.

WHAT KIND OF RIDER ARE YOU?

Where on the continuum of cycling enthusiasts do you find yourself? Read the following descriptions of four basic categories of riders—Fitness, Event, Competitive, and Racer—and decide which one best describes you as a rider right now.

Fitness rider. You ride for fun and fitness a few hours a week at most, whenever you can find the time. You want to maintain this fitness base, ride indoor or outdoor, and you might also ride to work or with groups as a social activity.

Event rider. You look forward to riding in one or more cycling event every year. You typically ride from six to fifteen hours a week. You want to improve your fitness and your skills on the bike so you can finish strong in each event.

Competitive rider. You are motivated to get faster and go farther. You ride fifteen hours a week or more, you like to make a good showing in your age group standings, and you are striving to reach the winner's podium.

Racer. You train twenty to thirty-five hours a week, with some weeks reaching fifty hours. Your goal is to win—period. You train to achieve the highest speed with the lowest risk of downtime and to maximize your abilities for peak performance on race day.

Did you recognize yourself in any of the four descriptions? Maybe you are straddling two categories. If so, bump yourself up to the next level and challenge yourself a bit. Although riders in all four levels will find useful information in this book, we have geared it particularly to the riders in the middle two groups: the event riders and the competitive riders. It is you folks who are goal-oriented, ready to take your training to the next level, eager to learn, and have the most to gain from a new way of riding—the Heart Zones way!

Whether you are an event rider or a competition rider, you are part of a new era, the first generation of riders who are discovering new ways to ride. Ushering out the old ways of riding takes a bit of courage. After all, most of us tend to gravitate back to what we know, to what is familiar, even when we know there is a better way. Enough of that! Muster up your courage—it is time to connect your riding to technology. In fact, there is no better way to take your training to the next level than to connect to the power of the one piece of technology that has transformed elite cycling—the heart rate monitor.

THE LANGUAGE OF YOUR HEART

The heart rate monitor lets you listen to your heart's voice and introduces you to the language of the heart. This numerical, dynamic language is beats per minute (bpm). It is astounding when you stop to think about it: You can hear the voice of your own heart through the monitor and see it displayed on a receiver on your wrist or on your handlebars. Even so, you might ask, "How can a changing number be a language?" If the purpose of language is to communicate, then bpm is very much a language, for this ever changing number communicates to you clearly and precisely what is happening internally. It is the summation of all of your internal responses to stress: external sources of stress such as hot weather and high altitude, and internal sources of stress such as dehydration and muscle fatigue. You are able to listen to the voice of your own heart and to understand what it is experiencing through a number on your heart rate monitor. Now, that is truly amazing!

USHERING OUT THE OLD WAY

Are you riding the new way or the old way right now? Find out by taking the self-assessment test in Table 1.1.

TABLE 1.1   Self-Assessment: The Old Way versus the New Way

Old Way? Check here	✔	New Way? Check here	✔
I don't use a bike computer.	☐	I use a heart rate monitor and a bike computer.	☐
I don't use any zones to train because I can feel how hard I am riding.	☐	I use zone training protocols and methodology.	☐
I use formulas such as "220 minus my age" to determine my training zones.	☐	I use submax tests or threshold tests to anchor my Heart Zones training zones.	☐
I follow the training plan that a friend gave me.	☐	I use an individualized and personalized training plan that I or my coach developed.	☐
I use low-intensity exercise to burn more fat.	☐	I measure my heart rate to become a better fat burner.	☐
I don't take any tests to see if I am improving on the bike.	☐	I take regular tests to measure fitness levels to see if I am getting stronger.	☐
No pain, no gain—that's the way I train.	☐	I vary my training to get better on the bike.	☐
I don't need to recover. I think it is important to maintain a high training volume.	☐	I know that I need recovery days and regeneration or transition periods.	☐
I don't use a heart rate monitor because I know my heart rate.	☐	I need a heart rate monitor to keep me in my heart rate zones.	☐
I train pretty randomly; I try to get a minimum amount of exercise per week.	☐	I measure and quantify my training load.	☐
I don't set goals—I just never get around to it.	☐	I set goals—it motivates me and guides my training.	☐

What was the final tally? If you put a lot of check marks in the Old Way column, listen up! You can transition out of those old ways and bring in the new ones. Embrace this new riding system and its companion tools—they are exactly what you have been looking for.

BRINGING IN THE NEW WAY

In the past, most coaches and cycling experts have looked at you, the rider, as a one-dimensional entity. They primarily cared about your physical skills and performance on the bike. Fortunately, those days are gone. Heart Zones Cycling is based on a multidimensional concept of you, the rider. This "whole cyclist" training framework begins with the realization that factors off the bike affect your riding on the bike. In other words, what happens to you when you are not riding plays a big role in how well you can train and race.

In this new way to ride, the person at the center of it all is you—the whole rider. In this new way to train, you take into account all of the events and conditions, what we call "training influencers," that can affect your riding performance. Training influencers comprise the global picture of your cycling environment—your training *framework* (see Figure 1.1).

Your training framework is the complete, global, holistic picture of all aspects of you, the rider, as a whole athlete, together with the external and internal factors that influence your training. You are at the center of this framework, and all of the elements and conditions that can influence your riding are also part of the framework. Each of the training influencers, working separately and together with all the other influencers, affects your performance on the bike. What happens to your race performance if you have been worried about the health of a loved one or work deadlines have deprived you of sleep the week before the race? Do you perform as well in the cold as in the heat? In rugged terrain as on flat city streets? Recognizing the interplay among all of the elements in your framework can help you understand how they affect your riding performance.

Remember, both you and your heart are interconnected to all the other factors in your global framework. That is why listening to your heart can give you insight into your physical and emotional health. Thinking in this new way, embracing the interconnectedness of your internal environment with your external environment, can lead to enormous results: increased speed, improved strength, better endurance, and a more emotionally satisfying experience on the bike.

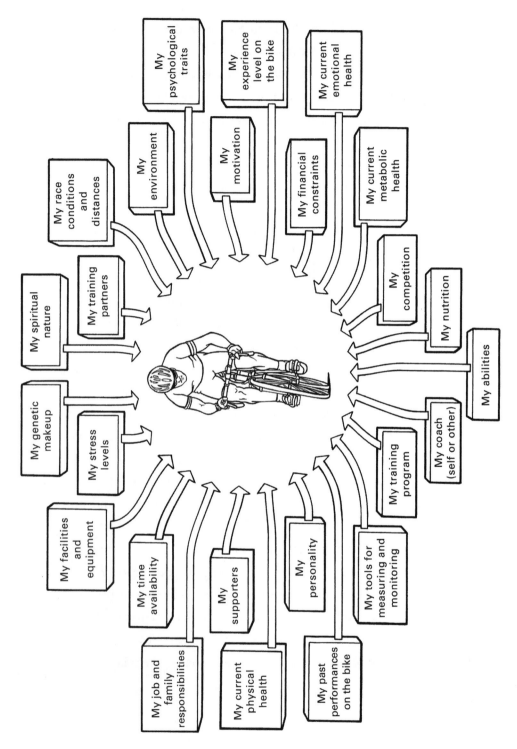

FIGURE 1.1 Training Influencers

TEAM AS PART OF YOUR FRAMEWORK

Some of the most important training influencers are the members of your team. It takes a team of informed, willing supporters to accomplish a big goal. The team members need a lot of information to support your efforts. Be sure to let them know everything there is to know about your goals. Probably most important to *them* is why this goal is important to *you*. Let them know the value of their contribution: When they let you ride in their slipstream, prepare meals for you and your family, take care of your children, and hold down the homestead, it is essential that you let them know how much you appreciate and respect their support.

Your team members need your direction so they can do their jobs. When they see the collective purpose, it binds them together in this cooperative effort. Tasks should be structured so that each person on the team knows his or her role and is empowered to play his or her part.

Who will be the head of your team? Some athletes like to take charge and be a self-coached rider. Others decide to hire a specialist, a coach or trainer, who will be in charge. If you decide to hire a coach, screen carefully. Fitting the right coach to the right athlete can be challenging.

THE NEW LANGUAGE OF CYCLING

If you have done much reading on training and racing, you know that it can be a confusing jumble of concepts and language. This confusion exists for many reasons. In part, it is a problem of terminology: coaches, athletes, teachers, and exercise scientists sometimes assign different definitions to the same words, or they assign the same definitions to different words. Toss in the translation of scientific findings from one language to the next, and it is no wonder the riders of the world are confused.

In order to get us all on the same page and speaking the same language of cycling, it is time to clarify a few terms that you will see often in this book, along with a description of how they are used in Heart Zones Cycling. (Check the Glossary at the back of the book for more Heart Zones Cycling terms.)

Training. (1) A program of physical activity designed to improve the skills and fitness capacities of an individual. (2) Any sustained exercise done at a heart rate or intensity level sufficient to result in metabolic adaptation in the muscles involved.

Training framework. The complete, global, holistic picture of all aspects of the rider as a whole athlete, together with the external and internal factors that influence the rider's training.

Training methodology. The big picture; the belief system behind Heart Zones Cycling and all the other Heart Zones Training programs (running, cycling, cross-country skiing, etc.). The Heart Zones Training methodology is built on twelve principles of training.

Training principles. The guidelines and rules that are built into Heart Zones Training that direct all aspects of this training methodology.

Training program. The particular method, as defined by an anchoring heart rate (maximum or threshold), by which Heart Zones Cycling is carried out by each individual rider.

Training plan. The document that embodies the ride schedule; the list of rides—what the rider does day-to-day.

HEART ZONES TRAINING METHODOLOGY

Heart Zones Cycling is a subset of the broader Heart Zones Training methodology. Understanding the Heart Zones Training methodology is essential to you as a rider. It is the starting point, the kickoff of your training. It is what you are going to follow, do, act, and be throughout your training time. The Heart Zones Training methodology involves two main aspects: the core procedures that make up the basic outline of Heart Zones Training and the twelve training principles that form its foundation.

Heart Zones Training Core Procedures

Common to all applications of Heart Zones Training are the following seven core procedures. These procedures also constitute the seven steps in your personalized training program. They are as follows:

1 Define your goals.
2 Determine your anchor heart rate.
3 Set your heart zones.
4 Periodize your training load.
5 Design your training plan.
6 Log your rides, your progress, and your thoughts along the way.
7 Assess and adjust.

Heart Zones Training Principles

The belief system behind Heart Zones Training is this: Training must be tailored to the unique attributes of each individual athlete. You, the athlete, can reach your highest maximum performance potential by listening and responding to the voice of your own heart, the most powerful indicator of your ever changing physical and emotional health.

Like most belief systems, Heart Zones Training rests on a set of principles. Twelve principles of training form the foundation of the Heart Zones Training methodology (see Table 1.2). Taking the time now to understand these principles will greatly enhance your ability to apply them when developing your own unique training program. The first three principles are at the center of this methodology: heart, zones, and training.

PERSONIFYING THE PRINCIPLES

Live by your training principles. When someone asks you, "Why are doing that?" you can explain that it is in keeping with your training principles.

TABLE 1.2   Heart Zones Training Principles

1	HEART	The heart (the physical heart and the emotional heart) is the center of cardiovascular training.
2	ZONES	Multiple heart rate zones lead to multiple benefits.
3	TRAINING	Heart Zones Training is a physical and emotional activity that is goal based.
4	MANAGEMENT	Heart Zones Training is a management system that allows you to measure and monitor your rides.
5	LOAD	Heart Zones Training is a way to track physical and emotional stress load, which leads to optimum physical and emotional performance.
6	UNIVERSAL	Heart Zones Training applies to all people, all sports activities, and all training systems.
7	INDIVIDUALIZED	Heart Zones Training is a personal approach that is designed for each individual.
8	TECHNOLOGY	Heart Zones Training uses training tools—technologies—that enhance the training experience and motivate the athlete.
9	INTENSITY	Heart Zones Training uses effort as measured by physical and emotional intensity to design the training program.
10	SYSTEMS	Heart Zones Training has several different approaches to training, each one anchored in a different way to measure intensity.
11	HARMONY	Heart Zones Training is built on finding the activities and events that resonate with you and your heart to create an active and healthy life. This is also known as entrainment.
12	PASSION	Heart Zones Training is centered on the discovery that we organize and execute around the passions of the heart.

Share these principles of training with others; most are riding without them. Use your training principles to get connected to your inner reasons for training and find harmony in your rides.

With time and practice, you might even reach a point of entrainment. What is entrainment? *Entrainment* is the riding experience when the mind, the body, and the emotions come together as one. It is the deepest connection between you and the bike.

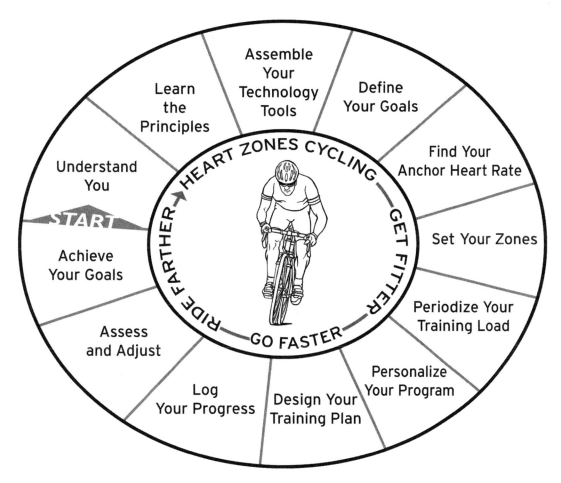

Figure 1.2 Around the Heart Zones Cycling Track

How do you get from where you are today to that experience of entrainment? Take a look at Figure 1.2. As you can see, you have just begun your ride around the track. You are beginning to think about your framework and your influencers, and you have been introduced to the principles of the Heart Zones Cycling methodology. Now you are ready to assemble your technology toolbox, which is discussed in the next chapter.

TOOLS
FOR RIDING

2

Having the right technology tools in your cycling toolbox is central to the Heart Zones way of training. When you connect your heart to a monitor, when you listen and respond to the beat, and when you apply data to your training system, you are using training technology tools as they were intended. Surprisingly, few riders use training tools, and fewer still understand them. An extremely small number use them to full advantage for systematic management of their training. You are about to become one of the fewest of the few!

Plus, tools are just plain cool. Even if all you do is watch the numbers go up and down on your heart rate monitor or power meter and wonder what the numbers mean, the data are fascinating to watch.

However, you are ready to take it a step further. You are ready to use your tools for diagnostics, for training management, for injury prevention, for emotional connections, for the power of motivation, for logging, and for analysis of your training plan. Tools give you insight into your health, fitness, and performance capacities.

You already know that tools give you data. Data can be viewed in real time or delayed time, adjusted (smoothed out over time, for example), and stored for later recall. Tools measure the following things:

Physiology. Body temperature, heart rate, sweat rate, blood lactate level, and oxygen consumption.

Stress. Ambient heart rate, delta heart rate, and anticipatory heart rate.

Position. Descent and ascent rates, latitude and longitude, and directional information.

Activity. Speed and pace, distance, and elevation changes.

Time. Event time, elapsed time, split time, and lap time.

Tools allow you to measure change. Take, for example, positional data. Monitors that use global positioning satellite (GPS) technology can tell you where you are and what your altitude is. By analyzing data collected over time, you can see any altitude changes or directional changes you made, as well as the route you took along the way. You cannot get lost if you have a GPS tool!

Tools can provide feedback in real time. For example, a heart rate monitor measures the slightest changes in heart rate in response to environmental changes. Tools also give you numbers that can be expressed as relative data (for example, a percentage of maximum heart rate), as absolute data (such as 50 watts of power output), and as units (pace in minutes per mile, for example).

You need tools, so get ready to go shopping!

YOUR SHOPPING LIST

Here are the three tools that you should put on your shopping list: a heart rate monitor, a GPS device, and a power meter. The heart rate monitor is essential. You will want the other two as well because they provide powerful data that will enhance your training. Each of these tools provides event riders and competitive riders the data they need in order to optimize their performance on the bike.

Tool 1: Heart Rate Monitor

This cardiac measurement tool uses advanced algorithms, integrated circuits, and signal-processing software to capture in beats per minute the rate of contractions of the heart muscle. A heart rate monitor measures the cardiac cost of an event, whether it is a 100-mile ride or a horror movie. A heart rate monitor is the body's personal tachometer: It does not tell you how fast you are going; rather, it tells you your cardiac muscle's response to internal and external loads.

FIGURE 2.1
Heart Rate Monitor and Transceiver

Heart rate monitors come in different shapes, sizes, and types (see Figure 2.1). Most resemble and are worn like a wristwatch. You may also know them as hand contacts on health club cardiovascular equipment such as rowing ergometers, elliptical machines, electronic stationary bikes, and treadmills.

HEART RATE MONITOR VERSUS PULSE METER

Heart rate monitors are different from pulse meters. A heart rate monitor uses the electrical signal from the heart's contraction as the source of the data, while pulse meters use biomechanical movement of blood through the arteries to assess heart rate data. Pulse meters are less accurate, often do not work well outdoors because they use a light sensor that can be disrupted with natural lighting, and are sensitive to movement. A heart rate monitor is a better choice.

Purchasing a heart rate monitor is similar to buying any other electronic device such as a computer, personal digital assistant (PDA), or mobile phone.

When you begin the shopping quest, decide on which functions you need and which features you want.

We suggest the following *minimum requirements* to look for in a heart rate monitor:

- Current heart rate
- Average heart rate
- Percentage of maximum heart rate and/or percentage of threshold heart rate
- Time in multiple heart rate zones
- Chronograph functionality

Are the preceding functions all you need? To start, yes. But you will soon crave more information to help you continue to get better on the bike. On the other hand, twenty-five years using monitors has taught us that it is probably better to start by buying less, not more. That is, get what you need now, not what you might need in the future.

To help you decide on what your needs and wants might be, consider your answers to these ten questions (it is OK if some of your answers at this point are "I don't know"):

1 What functions do I need now?
2 What features do I want now?
3 How may my needs grow?
4 What is my budget?
5 How much programming of the monitor am I willing to learn?
6 Are maintenance, repair, and warranty issues important?
7 Do I want to download my data into a computer, or do I want to see the data on the monitor?
8 Am I the kind of person who just wants to put the monitor on and use it without programming it before each workout?

9 Am I going to take the time to learn how to use my monitor, to read the user's guide, and enjoy information like recovery heart rate, time in zones, heart zones training points, or heart rate lap data?

10 Am I a gadget gal or guy who loves all the bells and whistles of personal training tools?

With those questions in mind, have a look at Table 2.1 for some of the features and functions you might find in today's heart rate monitors.

When looking at heart rate monitors, you may notice a number of different terms applied to these appliances: weight loss monitor, fitness monitor, runner's monitor, cycling monitor, and so forth. A cycling monitor, for example, might include functions such as heart rate, speed, altitude, temperature, cadence, riding time, and power output. Do not focus so much on the name of the monitor but rather on what it does.

Downloading heart rate monitor data. Before you purchase a monitor, you need to know that there are two ways to get data out of your heart rate monitor and into a log, spreadsheet, or software program. The first method is tried and true and a little "old school": You look at your monitor and write down the numbers in your cycling log or enter the numbers into a software program. The second way is to perform an electronic download: Send the data from your monitor directly to the software program via wireless communication or a cable. Computer-based downloading of workout data into a heart rate workout profile and summary information can be one of the most interesting features of a training monitor. This summary data is invaluable in measuring fitness improvement and permanently recording your rides, because it allows you to use the stored data for postride interpretation and evaluation. Decide which method of downloading data you will use before you venture out to buy a new heart rate monitor.

Ready to shop? There are nearly 200 different models of heart rate monitors made by more than twenty manufacturers. Each type of monitor has

TABLE 2.1 Heart Rate Monitor Functions and Features

Heart Rate Functions	Recording Functions
Current heart rate*	Switch function mode to transmitter by touch
Average heart rate*	Recovery features time in multiple zones*
Percentage maximum heart rate*	Peak heart rate
Percentage threshold heart rate	Fat burning estimation
Zone alarm: audible or visual	Time above and below a zone
Zone ceiling and floor settings	Total exercise time
Time in zone(s) memory	Memory time interval settings (5, 20, and 60 seconds)
Peak heart rate	Display workout results as bar or profile graph
"Within zone" bar	Interval settings with and without heart rate
Calorie estimation, cumulative calories	Recording rates for heart rate samples
Heart zone estimation	Dynamic memory stores and displays of the last few workouts
Oxygen consumption estimation	Recording altitudes
Sum of training load (Heart Zones Training Points)	

* Mandatory function for Heart Zones Cycling

different functions and features and has its own methods of programming or "button-pushing." At Heart Zones, we call this button-pushing "buttonology." Buttonology is the art of figuring out which buttons to push on your monitor to get the functionality that you want. As you select monitors with more functions and features, you add more buttonology, which typically increases the cost of the tool.

As with other electronic products, monitors are going through a "convergence" product cycle—two or more discrete technologies converging in one device. For example, you can get a cell phone that also has heart rate functionality. Look for heart rate technology in MP3 players, PDAs, and other training tools such as power meters, GPS devices, and metabolic meters.

TABLE 2.1 Heart Rate Monitor Functions and Features *(continued)*	
Additional Features	*Data Download Method*
Lap timing with heart rate, including best lap time; lap and split times; current average and peak heart rate for each lap; samples saved at preset intervals; no chest strap required	Manual recall
	Infrared
	Sonic link
	Two-way linking
Water resistant or waterproof	Direct link to download box
Multiple display options	Data recording device
Easy-to-read digits	
Wireless transmission	*Watch Functions*
Toggle between audible/silent alarm	Zoom (enlarges display)
Comfortable and aesthetically pleasing	Distance + heart rate
Backlighting	Help key*
Fitness tests	Time of day
User's personal ID, name, logo	Alarm
Selection of measurement units	Countdown timer
Display options	Count-up timer
Upload data and setting	Calendar
Ease of programming with pointers or text	Single and cumulative exercise time

Once you are using the monitor that meets your needs, wants, and budget, you will find no better aid to support your personal training. To learn more about heart rate monitors and to do some online comparisons, go to our Web site, www.HeartZones.com.

Tool 2: DASH© (GPS) Meter

DASH is an abbreviation that we at Heart Zones like to use; it stands for Distance + Altitude + Speed + Heart Rate. DASH meters use GPS technology.

GPS 101: A cyclist's guide to satellites. The Global Positioning System is a network of satellites that were put into space orbit by the U.S. Department of Defense to be used for military purposes. In the 1980s, the U.S. government granted international access to the GPS network for civilian purposes. Now a variety of applications from smart bombs to automobile navigation systems routinely use GPS technology. GPS works 24/7, anywhere in the world, and in any weather conditions.

In the GPS network, a constellation of 27 satellites (including three that serve as backups) orbit 12,000 miles above the Earth. Each of these two-ton solar-powered satellites makes two complete orbits around the Earth every day. The orbits are arranged so that at any time, anywhere on Earth, at least four satellites are "visible" in the sky. The satellites send signals at the speed of light, which is 186,000 miles per hour (300 million meters per second), to five different ground stations located in different parts of the world.

Meanwhile, your wrist-top or handheld GPS tool consists of two parts: a sensor that connects with the satellites and a receiver that receives the data and interprets your location.

In order to work, the GPS sensor must "see" at least three satellites. If the sensor or transceiver drops sight of one or more of the satellites because, for example, you went indoors or rode under a canopy of trees, a message appears on the display telling you that the signal has been dropped. When the signal is clear of obstruction, it adjusts for the dropped signal, synchronizes with the new location, interprets the new navigational fix, connects with the other "bread crumbs" or way points, and you rarely lose your trail during the lost signal time.

Current GPS technology works only outdoors because of the requirements for the GPS sensor to connect in a direct line of sight with satellites. When strapping on the device, keep the sensor clear of obstructions such as the frame of the bike, apparel, and other items that might block the sending and receiving of signals.

Using a mathematical process called *trilateration*, your GPS sensor figures out where you are based on the location of at least three satellites above you and the distance between you and each of those satellites.

The satellites pinpoint or triangulate your exact position on Earth and signal back the latitude and longitude coordinates to the receiver, called a *transceiver*. This triangulation provides your DASH monitor with "positioning data." This positioning data is processed by the transceiver into relevant data such as speed on the bike, your exact location, and your altitude. Since way points (navigation fixes) can be stored, this device can also serve as a navigational tool to give you a route back to your starting point or to directional coordinates that you provide.

Your GPS transceiver then displays your position anywhere on (or above) the Earth, usually to within three feet of accuracy. As long as you have a clear view of the sky and your GPS tool, you will never be lost again.

You have lots of choices when it comes time to download your GPS data. There are client-based and Web-based solutions; some are free, and others require that you pay a fee. The tool itself is usually packaged with the manufacturer's GPS software, and excellent third-party solutions are also available.

DASH: GPS and heart rate combined.   The tools we call DASH monitors, in which GPS technology is joined with a heart rate monitor in a single tool, are examples of the convergence of technology. Manufacturers are quickly inventing all kinds of convergences, so we are already beginning to see bike computers with GPS, cell phones with GPS, PDAs with GPS, and, of course, MP3 players with GPS. Soon all of this technology will converge into a single wrist-top appliance that is connected 24/7 to the Web.

Buying GPS tools, with or without heart rate functionality, requires some research. Because the technology is new in the cycling application, new products are rushing to the market. We want to avoid dating ourselves by not providing you with recommendations of models, features, and functionality that might be here today and gone tomorrow. Just make sure you do your homework.

Tool 3: Power Meter

Power meters measure the force or the work that you are exerting on the pedals. Different power meters use different methods of measuring this force. One popular way of measuring power is to use a strain gauge mounted in the hub of the rear wheel or on the crank arm. Strain gauges measure the torsion or twisting on the metal parts as force is applied and translates these data into power measurements. The power output data is then displayed on a monitor mounted on the handlebars. The data are displayed continuously and stored for later retrieval and analysis (Figure 2.2).

Another method used by equipment manufacturers, though not as precise, is to measure chain vibration. This vibration is then translated into watts to estimate power output.

FIGURE 2.2
SRM Power Meter Crank

Power meters are the preferred training tool of competitive cyclists because they measure exactly what these cyclists need to know—force over time. Having the ability to track power improvements may be the most important element for improving your cycling performance. Riders can now accurately determine their strengths and weaknesses, make the correct changes to their training program, and also know with certainty that their hard work is paying off with true fitness improvements. Many factors in cycling can determine the winner of a triathlon or bicycle race, but usually the rider who can apply the highest force over the longest period throughout a competition wins the race.

Power meters measure your wattage, which is the product of how fast you are pedaling (rpm) and how hard you are pedaling (the amount of force that you exert on the pedal), which on the bike means that you can produce more wattage either by pedaling at a harder gear at a slower rpm or by pedaling an easier gear at a faster rpm. To generate the most power, you pedal at the highest gear that you can push (force) at the highest cadence. More power means faster speed on the bike.

Downloadable power meters are valuable training tools. According to Hunter Allen, coauthor of *Training and Racing with a Power Meter*, "They let you make objective comparisons of your workout by recording wattage, cadence, speed, and heart rate data for each workout, track your fitness changes over time, and easily determine your strengths and weaknesses over the course of your training season."

Because power data can be difficult to interpret and apply to training, riders are encouraged to become educated about this topic, including how to use data analysis software, in order to realize the full potential of power meter training.

GET THE MOST FROM YOUR TOOLS

Here are a few tips to help you select the right tools, keep them in good working order, and use them to their full potential.

Get the functionality and features that are right for you.
Download capability. Does the device have the capacity to download to the Web or to a client for data analysis and interpretation?

Real-time data. Does the tool display the data in real time as you are working out?

Relative and absolute data. Does the monitor let you see both the relative number (such as percentage) and the absolute number?

Internal or external data storage. Is the data stored within the device that has the display or in a second device that records it?

Programmability. Can you program the monitor and put in your unique physiological information such as threshold heart rate or peak power output?

Convergence. Does the tool collect and/or display more than one type of data, such as a heart rate monitor that is a power monitor as well?

Expense. If you spend more money, do you get more functions and features?

Read the manual. This is a very important but frequently ignored tip: Read all of the documentation that comes with your tool. It is worth taking the time to learn to use your meters and monitors. You may wish to keep your manual with you for the first week so you can refer to it as often as you like. After you have worked with the monitor and the manual together for a while, you will find it easy to get all of the information you want. Try not to get frustrated with the manual. Just take your time and learn about your new tools step-by-step.

The one-week (or one-month) rule. If you are new to Heart Zones Training, do not expect to grasp how to make your monitors work for you the very first day. It takes time. Be patient with yourself. Give yourself a week of using your monitor, and you will fall in love with the power of the information it provides. OK, maybe it will take more than a week if you have a multifunctional tool. In that case, take one month and stay focused on using it for every ride during that time.

Connections and links. This is the wireless age, the age in which different devices synchronize or connect with one another—transmitters connect to receivers and transceivers connect with satellites. So, before you take off for a ride, make sure that your monitoring devices are synchronized.

Become a data aficionado. Learn what the numbers on your monitor mean, including intensity, energy output, internal and external stresses, location and distance, substrate utilization, and the force that you are applying to the pedals. Let the data serve as your coach, your motivator, your reference point, and, most of all, your friend. Become an expert at data interpretation, and apply what you learn to manage your riding plan and raise the bar of your riding and racing.

Trust the monitor.   People frequently tell us that they think their monitors are broken because the numbers do not seem right. Invariably, the monitor is correct and the rider is wrong. It is easy for a rider's perception of energy expenditure or intensity level to be inaccurate. Environmental, social, physiological, neuromuscular, hormonal, psychological, and emotional factors have an enormous impact on your perception of exertion. That is why you need a monitor.

Your monitor is a management tool, not a speedometer.   Some riders still use their heart rate monitors and their power monitors the old way, as speedometers. That is not the Heart Zones way. You will get greater benefit out of less training time when you use your tools systematically to train in an effort to accomplish a goal. Convert your training tools into power tools by making them essential parts of your "management system."

Do regular maintenance on the tool.   You clean your bike and do regular bike maintenance, checking your tires, brakes, and cables frequently. Do the same with your training tools. Make sure that they are calibrated. Do not misuse them. For example, do not push any of the buttons on your heart rate monitor when it is underwater—it increases the risk of leaking. Upgrade your software regularly. Look for new third-party software to complement your tool and give it more power.

Check battery levels.   Changing the battery is a task best left to the manufacturer or a specialist. Your manual or manufacturer's Web site will tell you where to send the monitor to have a battery replaced or other repairs done. Frequently check the battery levels of your training tools—it is disappointing to be in the middle of a race and have your monitor die.

Get the accessories.   Many useful items are available that will help you fully enhance and enjoy your meters and monitors. Get them. Books and videos on training with these tools help you get past the learning curve quickly. Take seminars or workshops, particularly ones that help you apply the tool to your needs and goals. How can you extend the application of the tool to other parts of your fitness training? How do you best use your monitor when cycling, for stress reduction, weight loss, or general fitness? Subscribe to newsletters that help you stay current in cycle training, event performances, and racing.

WHAT THE FUTURE HOLDS

You can already get cycling monitors that feature positioning (latitude and longitude), speed, altitude, thermometer, cadence, riding time, and power output—all in one tool. Yet technology is changing rapidly. As the speed of technological change increases, tools continue to provide more features and more functions. New tools are being developed that soon may have consumer applications such as portable gas analyzers that can provide continuous data on your oxygen consumption while you are cycling or running. Swift advancements in sensing devices are being made to capture the data and transmit it to a device that displays and stores it. Wireless connectivity and convergent technologies are leading to exciting technological innovation. Even cell phones are now receiving data from fitness tools and being used to transmit this data to Web servers.

Fabric technology is also evolving quickly. Biophysical fabrics act as sensors for heart rate monitoring, positioning, and motion, and some feature textile antennas and electromagnetic shielding.

Just as there is a new way to ride your bike, there are new tools to take with you. With each new year, there is a new generation of physiological measurement tools. We cannot wait to see what comes next!

DEFINING YOUR GOALS: AS EASY AS 1, 2, 3

No matter what term you want to use to describe it—*mission, purpose, dream, agenda,* or *goal*—the intent is the same: You want to accomplish something that has personal significance and relevance to you. You need a big goal to strive for, a target.

What is your big goal, and what part does your heart (your *emotional* heart) play in helping you achieve it? If your heart is not in it, do you think you are going to succeed? Probably not. If, on the other hand, your heart is connected to the reasons behind your goals, do you think you will succeed? Of course. Goals. Purpose. Heart. They are all interconnected; they make up the "flow," that frequent occurrence on the bike when it all comes together: You feel strong, the ride is effortless, and you are riding in the moment. Goals are central to Heart Zones Cycling; you simply cannot get better on the bike without them. That is why setting goals is the first fundamental step in the Heart Zones Training methodology.

GOALS ARE . . .

- the heart of motivation.

- the power behind drive.

- the muscles that pull us toward what we spiritually and emotionally want.

- what release the energy within us.

- powered by values and purpose that set the stage for action.

- what help us keep our eye on the prize—what help us concentrate and avoid distractions.

- the intentions that keep us on track.

WHO DEFINES YOUR GOALS?

It is best to be the author of your own goals. You need goals that pull you toward them rather than goals you are pushed into. Goals that come from the heart, the emotional heart, are the strongest of all. That is why you must write your goals. Then you can truly use your imagination to visualize yourself accomplishing those goals. Write them on the banner you see draped across the finish line in your dreams—your odds of achieving them will increase tremendously.

If goal setting is new to you, seeking help from a coach, trainer, nutritionist, psychologist, or other professionals can be extremely valuable. Get it. Pay for it. It is worth every nickel.

DEFINING GOALS IS A PROCESS

It takes preparation and knowledge to set meaningful goals. The preparation involves conducting an assessment of your physical and emotional status, your strengths and weaknesses on the bike, your time availability, and your resources. In essence, try to get a clear picture of all the aspects of you and your environment at the start of your training program. The knowledge you need in order to set meaningful goals comes from learning the characteristics of an effective goal, understanding the various aspects of motivation, and appreciating the importance of goals in your training program.

The process of creating meaningful and powerful goals has three parts: assess your baseline, determine your needs, and define your goals and put them in writing.

Assess Your Baseline

It is a basic fact of life: You have to know where you are now in order to figure out how to get somewhere else. It is just like getting driving directions online. You enter a starting address and a destination address, and a mapping Web site gives you the step-by-step plan on how to get there. No starting point, no plan. So, where are you right now?

It all starts with you, the rider. What is your current fitness level? You might think about getting a complete medical checkup. Invest in fitness measurements, and get a personal performance evaluation. What is your aerobic capacity? What is your threshold heart rate? What are your threshold speed and threshold power? What is your basal metabolic rate? What is your preferred source of fuels that you burn at low intensity and high intensity?

Next, think about your current skill level as a rider. List your skill strengths and weaknesses on the bike. Also think about your equipment and your support team. Take a mental snapshot of all the factors that come together to define you as a rider (in other words, your framework).

Finally, think about your experiences as a rider. With whom did you ride last year? In what events did you ride? How did you do? How much time do you devote to riding now? Do you have a training program, or have you been riding without a plan?

Write down your answers to all of these questions, and refer to your notes as you progress in your training program.

Determine Your Needs

Determine your needs as a rider by reviewing all the pieces of your cycling life and by figuring out those areas in which you would like to see change occur. What do you need to improve to do better in your events? Remember, Heart Zones Cycling is more than what you do on the bike; it also encompasses you as the person who is training in the context of your training framework. Are there indicators of your health and fitness that you would like to see improve?

Think about your skill level. Which new skills would you like to have six months from now, a year from now? Which skills would you like to improve in?

How about your equipment? What gear do you need to invest in to stay up with the competition? Who do you need on your team, and what skills do they need? Do you need to make more time for your riding, or set aside more financial resources?

Consider where and how you have been riding as well. Have you been challenging yourself? Are you bored with your rides? If you have been using a training program, in what ways was it not a good fit for you and your life? What do you need to change?

Put Your Goals in Writing

Before we go into great detail about how to write a goal that works, we want to say this loud and clear: "Write them down!" Goals that are not written down are not worth making. Do not point to your head and say, "They're all up here." Old-fashioned paper and pen work, computers work, whatever. Just make sure you write this stuff down.

WRITE SMART GOALS

Goals that work are SMART: specific, measurable, action-oriented, realistic, and timely. What do these traits mean?

Specific. Detailed descriptions of what, when, where, and how are in-cluded (or implied) in the goal statement.

Measurable. Data can be collected to verify that the goal was achieved.

Action oriented. The goal is a description of something you will *do.*

Realistic. Given the realities of your life and your training, you have the ability to accomplish the goal.

Timely. It is the right time in your training sequence and in the context of you and your framework to strive toward this particular goal.

Here are examples of SMART goals:

Short-term goal. Thirty days from now, complete twelve reps (up from nine) of isolated leg training (one rep is pedaling at 50–60 rpm with the left leg for 30–60 seconds, then recovering with both legs for one minute).

Longer short-term goal. Three months from now, increase average speed to 15 mph during a 20-mile time trial (up from 13 mph).

Shorter long-term goal. Complete the 45-mile ride from my house to City Hall (that includes two hills of about 5 percent grade) in under three hours.

Long-term goal. Twelve months from now, complete the North Shore Cen-tury in under six hours.

What makes them SMART? Each one pertains to a specific outcome that can be measured with verifiable data, they describe action-oriented targets that can be realistically achieved by the rider, and they occur at the correct time in the training plan.

Take a moment to practice writing short-term and long-term SMART goals right now:

- Short-term (30 to 90 days)
- Longer short-term (90 to 180 days)

- Shorter long-term (180 to 360 days)
- Long-term (one year and beyond)

Having trouble thinking of goals? Hop on your bike and go for a ride. You are sure to come up with some. Just remember to write them down!

YOU'VE GOT GOALS, NOW WHAT?

Now that you have a list of thoughtful, powerful goals, what do you do with them? Periodically, do three things: prioritize, evaluate, and adjust.

Prioritize. Organize your goals by priority so that you can better plan how to achieve them.

Evaluate. Analyze your progress along the way. Put "evaluation days" into your personal planner or calendar; have regularly scheduled meetings with your coach (or yourself!) to review your progress.

Adjust. Adjust your goals based on your evaluation. Is your data telling you that you are progressing faster than you expected? If so, up the ante—give yourself a more challenging goal.

WHAT'S THAT AGAIN?

The process of harnessing the power of goals is so important, we want to make sure you get it:

- Assess your baseline
- Determine your needs
- Define your goals and write them down
- Prioritize your goals
- Evaluate your progress
- Adjust your goals according to your data

FINE-TUNING GOALS WITH FEEDBACK

Feedback lets you know if you are marking time, falling behind, or moving toward your goals. Feedback comes in many forms, but for the cyclist in training, it means having data that shine light on your progress. These kinds of data come from training technologies such as heart rate monitors, distance-and-speed devices, and power meters. Setting goals, getting feedback, interpreting data, and making adjustments: It all adds up to riders getting faster and stronger, with better use of recovery periods along the way.

Goals without feedback have little effect on your motivation; feedback without goals has little effect on your motivation. But with clear goals that come from the heart and feedback data working together, you can manage your cycle training, you can monitor your progress, and you can measure your training improvements as you work toward your goal.

Goals and feedback—now, that's smart training!

HOW PAT BURTON ACHIEVED HIS GOAL TO LOSE 100 POUNDS

I was fat, just a biscuit away from 300 pounds. Holiday season 2001, I hit my breaking point. I had a holiday party to go to, and I had nothing to wear. Oh, I had plenty of decent clothes, but none of them fit. To go out and buy new clothes again would be to admit that I was fat again. I had been a frequent rider of the weight loss roller coaster. Been there, done that, got the T-shirt (which quickly became too tight on me).

So I changed my life. I set a goal to focus on my cycling and not on my weight.

A year later I had lost more than 100 pounds, reduced my body fat by more than 20 percent, and gone from a couch potato to a Heart Zones Green Jersey Indoor Cycling instructor. I learned how to eat and exercise, and, just as important, I learned what not to do.

I re-created myself at age 40.

The diet part came fairly easily for me. When I want, I can have ironclad willpower. But to make this a complete lifestyle change, riding had to play a major role. Even when I was stressing out the springs on the scale, I enjoyed cycling. I made that my main form of exercise. It is social and I enjoy it.

I set my goal to repeat the Six-Gap Century Challenge, a 100-mile bike ride over six of the highest mountain gaps in Georgia. The ride consists of 10,400 feet of climbing, and I had ridden it once before. I wanted to do it again, but it takes a lot of energy to haul 300 pounds up a mountain on a bicycle. My wife, Angie, has always supported me in everything I do, and this challenge was no different. It was Angie who introduced me to Heart Zones indoor cycling classes at Gold's Gym in Atlanta, Georgia, my home-town. I was a bit skeptical, but she told me an instructor named Joe would take me through a class that was "awesome"—and that I would want to "throw up" after fifteen minutes. Awesome and throw up: two terms that have not appeared together in a sentence of mine since my frat party days.

Soon thereafter, I meekly walked into Joe Domaleski's class. Joe, an Iron-man, was not what I had imagined. He was not this huge, towering drill in-structor type; instead, he used personal pride to drive your motivation. And after fifteen minutes, I did not feel like throwing up. Actually, I thought I was going to die. Yet I was hooked on riding indoors to train for an outdoor ride.

Joe was in the process of learning about Heart Zones Training, a training program that targets all your fitness heart rate zones using a heart rate monitor and specific indoor cycling training programs. It is a system that not only helped me with my weight loss goals but also put me on the fast track with my cycling fitness. After tasting what Heart Zones was about, I wanted more information. After several months of training with Joe, I at-tended a seminar and certification and became a Blue Jersey Level 1 trainer myself. I felt like my eyes had been opened. The information was pouring in: submax testing, delta tests, ambient heart rates, resting hearts rates, emotional fitness training in the heart rate zones, training in all my heart zones, and so forth. I felt like I was really equipped to make the final push to reach my goal of Six-Gap.

Heart Zones Indoor Cycling was not the first gym exercise routine I had started. It was, however, the first time I had a well-defined, clear, written goal that would require me to lose weight and become healthy. I knew I would not be able to do this alone; having a support team is very important. My support team seemed to grow with every pound I lost and every additional hour I spent exercising.

By the month of Six-Gap, my weight hovered around 200 pounds, yet I could climb with riders thirty pounds lighter than me.

I have become a force to be reckoned with! I am leading the pack up the hills and feeling great doing it. To Joe and everyone else on my side, all I can say is, "Thanks! I would not be here if not for you guys."

—Pat Burton,
Heart Zones Cyclist

YOUR ANCHOR
HEART RATE

4

Define your goals

▶ Determine your anchor heart rate

Set your heart zones

Periodize your training load

Design your training plan

Log your rides

Assess and adjust

After all the methodological, philosophical, goal-setting, commandment-pronouncing, in-your-head, off-the-bike conceptualizing in the previous chapters, you might be saying to yourself, "Philosophy and principles are fine, but I want to get on the bike!" If so, you are in luck because in this chapter, you will take the first step in applying what you *know* (the methodology) to what you want to *do* (get faster and stronger on the bike). That first step is determining your threshold heart rate or your maximum heart rate.

So far, you have learned about the Heart Zones Training methodology and the principles that form its foundation. Now you will learn how to apply the concepts, tools, and procedures of the methodology to your training framework in an individualized cycling training program. This program is going to be based on measuring, manipulating, and being responsive to the amount of effort or exertion your body is experiencing during training.

YOUR INDISPENSABLE TOOL, THE HEART RATE MONITOR

A heart rate monitor is a watchlike device that uses electrical signals from the heart muscle to measure the number of times per minute your heart contracts or beats per minute. You can find more information about heart rate monitors in Chapter 2, " Tools for Riding."

Heart rate serves as a very accurate indicator of athletic exertion or effort, and the best way to measure heart rate is with a heart rate monitor.

IS PULSE THE SAME AS HEART RATE?

You have probably had the experience of taking your pulse by placing your fingers on your wrist or the side of your neck and feeling the small thumping as the blood courses through your blood vessels. If you find yourself without a heart rate monitor, you can get an estimate of your heart rate by counting your pulse for six seconds, and then adding a zero to that figure to get beats per minute. Although taking your pulse in this way will get you through in a pinch, it is less accurate than the measurements taken by a heart rate monitor. By all means, get yourself a heart rate monitor.

ANCHORS AWAY!

The very name of the Heart Zones Cycling program gives away the two key concepts of the program: heart and zones. First, the program uses heart rate, which is a powerful window on the amount of stress (exertion or effort) your body is experiencing, and which can be easily measured.

Second, the program uses zones, which refer to ranges of heart rate measurements. Zones are defined in relation to a particular heart rate.

This particular heart rate number is the *anchor* of the program—an anchor because it serves as a stable reference point to guide your training. So how do you determine this heart rate, this very important anchor? Read on!

IS HEART RATE ALONE ENOUGH DATA?

In the 1980s, when wireless heart rate monitors first became available, they were the first tools that truly made a difference in health, fitness, and performance training. They changed training systems, created new methodologies such as Heart Zones Training, and for nearly two decades were the only non-laboratory performance tools available to riders. They were not cheap, costing well over $200 each, but to athletes serious about their training, they were worth every penny. What they could do for performance, stress reduction, weight loss, and motivation was phenomenal.

According to Carl Foster, PhD, one of America's most prominent applied exercise physiologists, heart rate monitors are incredibly powerful because they provide an amazingly simple way to get at complex physiological data. We realize that some coaches criticize the use of heart rate monitors for just that reason. Heart rate monitors combine a plethora of complex changes in the body into a single measurement. A heart rate monitor does not differentiate when the change in that number is the result of thermal changes, hormonal changes, nutritional changes, or exercise stress changes. However, we like how heart rate data sums up all of the changes in a precise and neat way and gives them to you in one elegant and simple number—beats per minute.

Say, for example, that in one moment, simultaneously, the temperature drops twenty degrees, humidity increases by 10 percent, you eat a packet of gel with 100 calories of pure sugar right after drinking a strong cup of java, you learn that the stock market dropped 300 points, you hear your dog snarling at the postal carrier, you are halfway through a series of standing five-minute sprint intervals on your indoor trainer, and you feel on the verge of getting a cold. In a single second, your body is experiencing a lot of complicated changes that it must regulate. What happens to your heart rate? Chances are, it goes up! As Foster says, your heart rate serves as an incredibly simple and elegant marker of very complex physiology. Your heart rate monitor shows immediate and continuous results; it becomes a powerful biofeedback tool in response to emotional, environmental, physical, hormonal, and metabolic stress.

Now, you could have used a half dozen different meters: thermometer, metabolic meter, stress monitor, power meter, and more. Or you could look at the numbers on your heart rate monitor and say to yourself, "This is elegantly simple." We think that for most riders, knowing all those separate numbers does not really help you get better on the bike. We know that by blending all of the data into one simple number, you can ride better than you ever have before. Heart rate alone gives you sufficient data to get the total picture. It forms the basis of the most comprehensive and effective system available for monitoring your training and racing.

MEASURING EFFORT THE HEART ZONES WAY

The Heart Zones Training methodology in all its permutations for all kinds of athletic training (walking, running, cycling, etc.) works equally well with any of several ways to define your anchor heart rate, including ventilatory threshold, maximum heart rate, lactate threshold, and maximum oxygen consumption. This book will focus on only two of the four: maximum heart rate and ventilatory threshold. However, if you are curious, you can learn a bit about other measurements of physiological effort at the end of this chapter.

Maximum Heart Rate

Maximum heart rate is exactly what the name says: the highest number of contractions your heart can make in a given amount of time, in other words, the highest number of beats per minute (bpm). Maximum heart rate is the easiest anchor point to use in the Heart Zones Cycling program because it is easy to assess using a heart rate monitor, does not change very much over time, and forms the basis of a program with five easy-to-understand heart rate zones.

It is important to note here that the tests to determine maximum heart rate do not include any of those seemingly simple formulas floating around. You have probably seen the one that says, "Maximum heart rate = 220 – age." Do not use this or any other formula to estimate maximum heart rate! Formulas are completely useless, and will lead you astray—a pretty important consideration, since the entire Heart Zones Cycling maximum heart rate program depends on the accuracy of your maximum heart rate measurement!

Maximum heart rate is one of the best anchor points; its only slight drawback is that it is sport-specific. Typically, but not always, maximum heart rate is highest in cross-country skiing and running, which are weight-bearing sports, and lower for cycling, which is a non-weight-bearing sport. If you are a multisport athlete, you need to assess your maximum heart rate for each of the sports in which you participate. No big deal.

It is pretty amazing, actually—maximum heart rate for each sport is a fixed number. It simply does not change no matter how fit you are. Get stronger on the bike, your maximum heart rate stays the same. Take time off the bike, your maximum heart rate stays the same. It is your heart's own unique fingerprint, and it is a very powerful piece of the training puzzle.

Ventilatory Threshold

Ventilatory threshold (from here on out, simply "threshold") is the point at which your body transitions from aerobic (sufficient amount of oxygen) metabolism to nonaerobic (insufficient amount of oxygen). This point, when your body begins burning carbohydrates without the use of oxygen, is known as the cross-over point and generally corresponds to between 75 and 85 percent of a fit rider's maximum heart rate. The fitter you are, the higher your threshold.

As a rider, what are you experiencing at your threshold? It means you have been riding with a high level of intensity, and you have reached a point of exertion at which speech is no longer comfortable. Because it is the first

MAXIMUM HEART RATE . . .

- is the highest number of times that your heart can contract in one minute (so it is measured in beats per minute).

- is genetically determined.

- is sport-specific.

- is a fixed number unless you become chronically unfit.

- is affected by many medications.

- does not predict athletic performance.

- does not reflect your current level of fitness.

- cannot be increased by training.

- cannot be increased by eating certain foods, getting stressed out, or drinking energy drinks.

- submax test results may be test-day sensitive, particularly if you are not properly rested before taking a maximum heart rate test.

- is altitude sensitive, decreasing about 1 bpm per 1,000 feet of elevation.

- varies greatly among people of the same age.

- cannot be estimated by using *any* mathematical formula.

- can be assessed relatively accurately by using submaximum testing protocols.

- can be sustained for only 15 to 45 seconds before you are forced to stop.

- has been measured as low as 155 bpm and as high as 240 bpm in adults.

- is higher in those with a small heart size or mass.

- is often higher in women.

- of an elephant is about 30 bpm and of a hummingbird is about 500 bpm.

- is the anchor point for setting the heart zones in the Heart Zones Cycling maximum heart rate program.

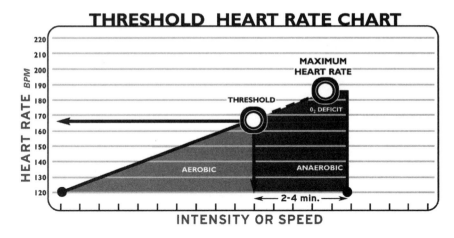

FIGURE 4.1   Threshold Heart Rate Intensity

point at which breathing becomes labored, it is known as the first ventilatory threshold, or VT_1. Figure 4.1 shows how threshold corresponds to heart rate on the continuum of riding intensity.

For a Heart Zones program anchored on threshold, it is important to identify your heart rate at the point at which your metabolism crosses over from aerobic to nonaerobic, which is the same point at which your breathing goes from easy to difficult. This threshold heart rate can be measured with great precision in the laboratory, or you can produce very good estimates with field tests.

TESTING TO FIND YOUR MAXIMUM AND THRESHOLD HEART RATES

Maximum heart rate is one measurement that can serve as the anchor point of your Heart Zones Cycling program, and threshold heart rate is another. Although several field tests are designed to help you determine one or the other of these figures, we have identified one test that serves to measure both—you get both your maximum heart rate and your threshold with a single test. In this test, called the Foster Talk Threshold Test, you first determine your

THRESHOLD HEART RATE . . .

- is the dividing point between aerobic and nonaerobic metabolism.

- is sport-specific.

- is one of the strongest predictors of athletic performance.

- is dynamic; it changes with fitness.

- is sensitive to test-day factors (fatigue, fuel, health status).

- is sensitive to equipment and laboratory factors.

- is a percentage of maximum heart rate that increases with better fitness.

- does not decline with age; it declines with declining fitness.

- is determined by fitness level.

- has great variability among similar individuals.

- cannot be predicted by *any* mathematical formula.

- testing requires the person to be fully rested, fueled, and ready to take the test.

- can be relatively accurately estimated doing field tests.

- is affected by at least four different factors: nutritional status, mode of exercise being used, the speed of the movements being made, and training status.

- decreases (is suppressed) with increasing altitude (about 1 bpm per 1,000 feet).

- increases with optimum training and decreases with overtraining.

- is a highly trainable heart rate anchor point.

- training improves the efficiency of both aerobic and nonaerobic energy-producing systems.

- can be identified by different methods in the field and in the laboratory.

- is the anchor point of the heart zones in the Heart Zones Cycling threshold heart rate program.

threshold heart rate, and then you calculate your maximum heart rate from that figure.

You will remember from our earlier discussion that your threshold heart rate is the heart rate associated with that moment during exertion when your body transitions from aerobic metabolism to nonaerobic metabolism; in other words, it is your first ventilatory threshold (VT_1). This transition can be ascertained by a shift in breathing patterns. As your riding speed increases, so does the stress on your cardiac system. Breathing frequency and depth shift to compensate for the greater demand for oxygen. The heart rate corresponding to the point at which this shift in breathing moves from a linear to a curvilinear pattern is your threshold heart rate.

Dr. Foster designed the Foster Talk Threshold Test after years of research on measuring ventilatory threshold breathing responses and corresponding heart rates. The aim of this test is to find the point at which talking begins to feel difficult and uncomfortable. It keeps you in a very safe zone, is easy to perform, and provides remarkably accurate results. It is best done on a calibrated exercise cycle. In addition, you will need a heart rate monitor and a selection of text that takes about thirty seconds to say out loud, such as the U.S. Pledge of Allegiance or another text of similar length. Before going into the details of the test protocol, we need to take a minute to explore the very important question, "Can you speak comfortably?"

"Can You Speak Comfortably?"

In the Foster Talk Threshold Test, there are only three acceptable answers to the question, "Can you speak comfortably?": "yes," "uncertain," and "no." Table 4.1 describes what those answers mean.

What is happening physiologically during the Threshold test? As exercise intensity increases, ventilation increases in a linear manner until you reach a certain intensity level called the "crossover" point. At the crossover intensity level, the ventilatory demands are greater than the ability of the oxygen

TABLE 4.1 Three Answers to "Can You Speak Comfortably?"

Answer	Explanation	Threshold?	Corresponding Heart Rate Number
YES	No undue stress on your breathing pattern. Can recite a 30-second passage with little effort.	Not yet	Prethreshold heart rates
UNCERTAIN	Not sure; equivocal. You are on the verge of not being able to talk. Saying a 30-second passage takes some effort.	First ventilatory threshold (VT$_1$)	Threshold heart rate
NO	Cannot talk comfortably. Called the negative stage. Typically, this is at or above 90% of maximum heart rate. You are unable to produce comfortable speech. You can not recite a 30-second passage without labored breathing. If you are a beginner, unfit, or returning to fitness, do not push yourself to this point.	Second ventilatory threshold (VT$_2$)	VT$_2$ heart rate

delivery system to meet those demands. At this intensity level—at this heart rate marker—ventilation increases exponentially rather than linearly. This intensity level is nearly identical to your lactate threshold. As Dr. Foster explains, "The discontinuity of linearity in either blood lactate accumulation or ventilatory patterns during incremental exercise represents a convenient marker of exercise training intensity" (Foster et al., 2006).

For our purposes, we are concerned only about the transition from comfortable breathing to not-so-comfortable breathing. In other words, we are interested in the point that you feel yourself crossing over from "yes" (you can speak comfortably) to "uncertain"; there is no need to go all the way to "no." The heart rate number associated with VT$_1$ is the anchor for the Heart Zones Cycling Threshold program; there is no need to find out your VT$_2$ heart rate number.

The Foster Talk Threshold Test Protocol

Tools and equipment needed. Calibrated exercise cycle (preferred) or studio bike, heart rate monitor, and thirty-second speech (such as the U.S. Pledge of Allegiance or a text of similar length).

Goal. Determine the heart rate corresponding to the transition from "yes," talking is comfortable, to "uncertain" whether talking is comfortable or not.

Procedure. At the beginning of each two-minute interval, increase your heart rate by 10 bpm, and maintain that heart rate for the entire two minutes. During the last thirty seconds of each interval, recite a thirty-second speech. Then, assess your ability to speak. See these steps in more detail below.

STEP 1. Warm up adequately for five to fifteen minutes.

STEP 2. Ride until you reach a heart rate of 120 bpm. Then, begin a series of two-minute intervals in which you increase your intensity by 10 bpm each interval.

STEP 3. Begin the first interval: Increase your intensity by 10 bpm, and maintain that intensity for two minutes.

STEP 4. In the last thirty seconds, while maintaining the same heart rate, recite the passage aloud.

STEP 5. After saying the speech, ask yourself, "Can I speak comfortably?"

STEP 6. Answer with one of the three acceptable responses: "yes," "uncertain," or "no."

STEP 7. Record your heart rate each time after answering the question.

STEP 8. Continue to increase your heart rate by 10 bpm for each subsequent two-minute interval, asking the question and recording your heart rate, until you have reached the heart rate at which you answer "uncertain."

STEP 9. Record your "uncertain" (VT_1) heart rate. This is your threshold heart rate.

STEP 10. To estimate your maximum heart rate, divide your threshold heart rate by 0.8. Your maximum heart rate (bpm) equals threshold divided by 80 percent.

Note: If extremely fit, divide your threshold heart rate by 0.85 rather than 0.80 in order to estimate your maximum heart rate; if developing fitness, divide your threshold heart rate by 0.75, or 75 percent.

TIPS FOR BETTER FOSTER TALK THRESHOLD TESTING

- Do the test at least two different times to reduce error. It can be done on the same day. Take at least a ten- to twenty-minute break between the two tests.
- Use a medium that is easy to control, such as a cycling ergometer or indoor power meter. This way, you can control speed more precisely and receive accurate electronic feedback.
- Consider using an experienced Heart Zones–certified trainer who knows the protocol to facilitate the test.
- If you are a multisport athlete, do the Foster Talk Threshold Test in each sport activity because threshold heart rate is sport-specific.

Periodically Retest

Chapter 8 provides three rides that you can use to verify and refine your measurement of maximum heart rate—Larger Than Life, Hill Sprints, and The All-Out Trip—and two rides that you can use to verify and refine your measurement of Threshold—Threshold Endurance Road Test and the Threshold Road Cycling Test. We recommend that you remeasure your threshold and your maximum heart rate periodically to make sure that you are working with an accurate value.

MAXIMUM OR THRESHOLD: CHOOSE ONE

In Heart Zones Cycling, you use a program based on either your maximum heart rate or your threshold heart rate, not both. Choose the one that you like the best. If neither one stands out, flip a coin to select one for this training season, and consider using the other one for your next training season.

OTHER WAYS TO SIZE UP EFFORT

There are several other indicators of physiological effort besides those measurable by field tests for threshold heart rate and maximum heart rate. Two of the best indicators are lactate levels in the blood and maximum oxygen consumption. Both of these are measured in laboratory settings.

Lactate is a salt substance produced from lactic acid, which is a product of muscle contraction. By measuring the lactate in your blood, you can determine the point at which your metabolism crosses over from aerobic (sufficient oxygen) to nonaerobic (insufficient oxygen). This lactate threshold is measured in a laboratory setting; blood samples are drawn periodically during exertion, and your blood lactate levels are measured.

Maximum oxygen consumption, also known as VO_2max, is the highest rate at which oxygen can be taken in and used during high-intensity dynamic exercise. This method for measuring exertion is considered by many exercise scientists to be the "gold standard" because it is both noninvasive and is measured with very accurate tools. VO_2max, expressed in milliliters of oxygen consumed per kilogram of body weight per minute, increases as your fitness improves. Like lactate threshold, it is measured in a laboratory setting.

Aerobic capacity is widely considered the most objective measure of endurance capacity. Your aerobic capacity, your VO_2max, gives you essential information about the capacity of your aerobic and nonaerobic energy systems. It is measured directly using a metabolic cart or indirectly doing submaximal testing. One of your primary training goals should be to get the biggest VO_2max that you can achieve, and Heart Zones Cycling can help you get it. Many factors contribute to aerobic capacity such as mitochondrial density, muscle fiber types, and capillary density, and they are all improved by spending time in the right zones on the bike.

Aerobic capacity is measured on a metabolic meter, a tool for training that is just now moving out of the exercise lab and into the marketplace in a way that coaches and trainers can more readily use it. The metabolic meter or metabolic cart measures important pieces of physiological data that are essential for intermediate to advanced riders. Data from metabolic meters includes the following:

VO$_2$max. Excellent indicator of your current fitness level, useful to compare with normative data, and useful as an anchor point to use to set percentages for training.

Metabolic threshold. Used to set training zones accurately based on precise measurement of the crossover point between aerobic and nonaerobic metabolism. Useful for creating individual rides within the training plan. Highly correlated between individual time trial performances.

Substrate utilization. The amount and kinds of fuels burned during exercise.

Power output. The amount of force that can be achieved at different speeds, at peak exertion, at threshold power, and at changes with different training protocols. Used for prescribing intervals based on a percentage of power output in watts.

ON THE CUTTING EDGE: HEART RATE VARIABILITY

- Elite athletes and their trainers are beginning to monitor heart rate variability (HRV) as the latest way to assess fatigue.
- HRV, which is the variation in the time between heartbeats, can serve as a very sensitive window into the physiological state of an athlete, and it can allow for the accurate tracking of fatigue and recovery.
- After the data downloads into specialized software for analysis, an athlete can see just how well his or her autonomic nervous system is responding to the stress of training, and whether there is any danger of overtraining.
- If you would like to learn more about this exciting new development in heart-centered training technology, contact a Heart Zones coach at www.HeartZones.com.

TABLE 4.2 General VO$_2$max Comparisons by Fitness Classification							
	Low	Fair	Average	Good	High	Athletic	Olympic
Female Ages 40–49	<25	26–31	32–40	41–45	46–50	51–56	57+
Male Ages 20–29	<38	39–43	44–51	52–56	57–62	63–69	70+

Source: Boulder Center for Sports Medicine, "Relative VO$_2$max Norms" handout. These are general, non-sport-specific, and not based on seasonal variations.

With this kind of data, coaches and trainers have a new way to design training plans and measure progress. They have a new way to prescribe exercise intensities and training zones and to assess fitness improvements. They know which fuels the rider is using at different levels of intensity and can recommend diet modifications to help the rider improve performance.

These kind of data let riders know more about their strengths and weaknesses. You can compare your aerobic capacity with others in your classification and see how you match up. Let's say that from testing, you learn that your VO$_2$max is 42 mL/kg/min. Without normative or comparison data, that number, 42 mL/kg/min., has little or no meaning, but compared to data from a year or two ago, you would be able see your improvement. You can also look at normative data and compare yourself to other cyclists. Table 4.2 shows relative VO$_2$max norms for men and women.

Knowing your VO$_2$max shows you the positive results from the training effect. For example, one study showed that in cyclists, a 20 percent change in VO$_2$max resulted in an improvement of 7 to 10 percent in finish times in a 26-kilometer individual time trial, and a 10 percent improvement in threshold heart rate decreased 26-kilometer individual time trials by approximately 4 percent (Olds et al., 1995).

You should also know something about the fuels or sources of calories you burn or metabolize (substrate utilization). The more efficient your fuel-burning capacity, the faster and farther you can ride. Your ability to oxidize fat efficiently spares carbohydrate stores. This is called *glycogen sparing.* Your ability to ride aerobically is almost limitless because your energy reserves, the calories that you have stored in your body, are on the order of 55,000 calories—enough for thousands of miles of riding. Even the leanest cyclists have an almost unlimited supply of stored fat but a limited supply of stored glycogen; you want to hold on to your glycogen stores until you need to call on them for high-intensity or duration performance.

Accurate identification of threshold power, threshold heart rate, and threshold percentage of VO_2max is extremely useful for planning training and competition strategies, but, unfortunately, metabolic assessment tests are not cheap. The equipment is expensive, and it takes an investment in time as well—about an hour for a certified metabolic specialist to administer the test and share the results with you. You are looking at $150 to $300 per test, with retests slightly less.

Of course, repeat tests are important because the information you need is how your numbers change over time. It is commonly recommended to take three to four tests a year depending on the periodization of your training. Tracking your test results is essential for you, the self-coached rider, to adjust your training and racing plan or for your coach to make recommendations to you about ways to ride and perform differently.

Metabolic testing requires a strict adherence to environmental and laboratory conditions that can affect the test results, such as humidity, room temperature, and barometric pressure, and proper calibration of the equipment is essential for accurate VO_2 results. Look for an experienced lab technician with proper certification or academic credentials.

Accurate metabolic testing results come best from those participants who have prepared for their tests. As an example, the individual taking the test should be familiar with the breathing apparatus, the bicycle ergometer, and the testing protocol. We would even recommend that you practice in advance of taking the test by doing a surrogate workout using the face mask in order to become familiar with the experience of it. Get comfortable with the testing equipment, usually an electronic bike or treadmill, and the mask in advance. Quite often, your rating of perceived exertion can be distorted when taking the test without familiarity of it because of the difficulty of inhaling and exhaling air through the mask. Read about the test protocol in advance to familiarize yourself with it.

A metabolic meter (metabolic cart) is an assembly of different pieces that together make up a metabolic testing system, also known as an *indirect calorimeter*. The two basic parts of the system are the volume-monitoring devices (volumetric equipment) and the gas analyzers (gas analysis equipment). The volumetric equipment measures the amount of inspired air (volume breathed in) and expired air (volume breathed out), and the rate and resistance of the flow of air. Modern metabolic carts use pneumotachographs to determine volume. These measure the decrease in pressure of airflow across a screen or through a tube and then convert this information mathematically from a pressure change to a volume. The result: The metabolic meter measures the amount of oxygen (VO_2) that you can extract from the air at different intensities by doing gas analysis with electronic oxygen and carbon dioxide analyzers.

A complete metabolic meter has a lot of pieces: the ventilation device, the oxygen analyzer, a PC, a printer, a portable stand, plus collateral gear such as a nose clip, a face mask, tubing, a heart rate monitor, and test equipment (treadmill, cycle, kayak or rowing ergometer). Because of the complexity of the system, coaches and laboratory exercise specialists have had difficulty getting accurate measurements in the nonlaboratory environment. If you want this kind of data (and we think you should get it), go to an exercise physiology lab or health club—your results, both in the lab and on the bike, will be well worth it.

PAUL'S MAXIMUM HEART RATE BIRTHDAY PARTY RIDE

Every year for my birthday, I like to ride 10 bpm over my maximum heart rate. Oh, you may say, "That is simply impossible because no one can ride over their maximum heart rate. You can only stay at your maximum heart rate for about fifteen to thirty seconds before you reach total exhaustion and your body forces you to stop."

Wrong.

There's more. I like to ride for an hour or more at 10 bpm and sometimes 20 bpm over my maximum heart rate, not twenty to thirty seconds. And now you may say, "I don't believe you, Paul, you are pulling my leg."

And I say the same thing to you again: Wrong.

But, first, let me tell you how I am able to ride above my maximum heart rate for such a long period of time.

As you may know, there are dozens of different arithmetic formulas that are popularly used even today to estimate maximum heart rate. Even though coaches and fitness professionals know they are obsolete, many of these experts still use them. In fact, there is no original research to substantiate any of these formulas. They are all incorrect, so folks are training in the wrong training zones and getting the wrong training results. Ever wondered why you aren't getting the training benefits that you are seeking? One of the reasons might be that you are training incorrectly.

I am living proof of that fact. I am now 87 years old. I have been field-testing my maximum heart rate for almost two decades. After reading Sally Edwards's pivotal best-selling book, *The Heart Rate Monitor Book* (1993), I followed her recommendation and did the "2- to 4-minute Maximum Heart Rate All-Out Test." Older people are not supposed to do this test, but I ignored that because I have been fit my entire life. When I first field-tested my maximum heart rate, I was 71 years old. At that time, my cycling maximum was 185 bpm.

Today, my maximum heart rate remains unchanged. It has probably not missed a single beat for all of these years. You know, I have to be honest. I didn't believe Sally when she first told me almost two decades ago that maximum heart rate doesn't drop with age. Even though Sally, my training partner for the past thirty years, said, "You know, Pinkhouse [that's my nickname because I live in a pink house—my wife selected the color], I think that after the age of 75 or maybe 80, your maximum heart rate might just drop. I might be forced to qualify my empirical research that maximum heart rate does not change with age unless one is chronically unfit." Well, I can provide the testimonial to her and to you; my maximum heart rate hasn't changed at all.

To celebrate each birthday—and they become more sweet and special with each one as I enter my tenth decade on this planet—I ride 10 bpm above my maximum heart rate as predicted by this popular equation: 220 – age = maximum heart rate. So this next December 26, my birthday, come along for the ride. I will average for an hour a heart rate 10 bpm over my arithmetic maximum heart rate of 130 bpm (220 – 90 = 130 bpm). In other words, I'll average over 140 bpm. That is in easy Zone 3 for me.

The point of my story is that the arithmetic formula to estimate maximum heart rate has too much error for anyone of any age to use. My maximum heart rate is 185 bpm. The formula says that it is 130 bpm. That is an error of 55 bpm. The formula has a deeper implication for me—it says that as you get older, you can train easier. It says that as you get older, you have permission to get less fit each year. The older I get, the more important it is for me to be fit. So don't believe the wall charts that say it is OK to get worse as you get older. It isn't.

Don't use the 220 – age = maximum heart rate formula. It is useless. Period.

—Paul Camerer,
Blue Jersey Level 1 certified trainer

SET YOUR
HEART ZONES

The concept of heart rate zones (or heart zones) is the central organizing idea of the Heart Zones Training methodology. A *heart zone* is a range of heartbeat rates expressed as percentages of your maximum or threshold heart rate. For example, one of the heart zones, Heart Zone 1, ranges from 50 to 60 percent of your maximum heart rate or 60 to 70 percent of your threshold heart rate. Structurally, a zone is like a room, with a ceiling, a floor, and space in between. And just like a room in a building, the ceiling of one zone is the same as the floor of the zone on top of it. The top of Zone 3, for example, is the same number as the floor, or bottom, of Zone 4.

All zones, whether in the maximum heart rate program or the threshold heart rate program, are a range of heart rates spanning 10 percent of each individual's sport-specific maximum heart rate or threshold heart rate. Each zone contains a "midpoint," which is located 5 percent from the top and 5 percent from the bottom of each zone. Midpoints are useful in training because they give you a nice target number. For example, a ride might consist of 10 minutes in each zone, which you could accomplish by aiming for the midpoint

TABLE 5.1   The Heart Zones Wellness Continuum

Zones	Wellness Continuum		
	Health Zones	Fitness Zones	Performance Zones
5			⇕
4		⇕	
3			
2	⇕		
1			

of each zone: 55 percent, 65 percent, 75 percent, and 85 percent of your anchor heart rate number.

Each zone is unique. What happens physiologically changes from zone to zone, such as the fuels consumed, how you feel while in each zone, the amount of time you can spend in each zone, and the training effect that results from spending time in each zone. For example, Zone 4 is where you begin to really improve your performance, but it is a tough zone to stay in for long periods of time, whereas Zone 2 starts your body on the road to metabolizing fat and is easy to spend time in.

The five heart zones fit together as part of what is called the "wellness continuum" (see Table 5.1). The wellness continuum means that the benefits from the zones fit into three different areas of wellness.

When training in the bottom three zones, the primary benefits are health benefits. When training in the middle zones, you earn fitness benefits. And if you want to achieve performance, most of your training takes place in the top three zones.

All zones are defined relative to an anchor point. That is, all zones are a percentage of your maximum or threshold heart rate. For example, in the maximum heart rate program, Zone 2 is 60 to 70 percent of your maximum heart rate. In the threshold heart rate program, Zone 2 is 70 to 80 percent of your threshold anchor point. In training, it is best to train by relative heart rate numbers rather than absolute heart rate numbers. That is, it is better to train knowing that you are riding at 70 percent of your maximum heart rate or at 80 percent of your threshold heart rate, rather than trying to reach and maintain a particular number such as 137 bpm.

You may be wondering if the benefits you get by spending time in the various zones are inclusive or cumulative. Unfortunately, they are neither. Training in Zone 4 does not give you the benefits of training in Zones 1, 2, and 3. You get only the physiological, metabolic, and emotional outcomes of a specific zone by spending time in that zone.

The following sections describe each of the zones in more detail. Each zone is associated with a color on various Heart Zones charts; the colors also represent the intensity of the workout in each zone, with blue signifying low intensity—"cool" and easy-going—green signifying a bit more intensity and therefore a little bit "warmer," and so forth.

ALL ABOUT ZONE 1, THE BLUE ZONE

Zone 1 is the kickoff point for those new to training. Riders new to cycling who are focusing on bike-handling skills and initiating a cardiovascular training regimen should spend lots of time in Zone 1. This is also the kickoff point of the wellness continuum because it is the first point where measurable aerobic benefits occur, such as the development of a healthier heart muscle. You do not burn a lot of calories, but those calories that you do burn come primarily from fat.

Zone 1 is 50 to 60 percent of your maximum heart rate, or 60 to 70 percent of your threshold heart rate. Hang out in Zone 1 and you will get a healthy heart, improve your metabolism, and experience all sorts of wonderful things happening to your emotions and your physiology. While you are riding in the Blue Zone, you can smell the roses, chitchat, and admire the scenery.

If you are in shape, Zone 1 is a great place for a gentle recovery ride. Training in Zone 1 improves metabolic fitness, including reduced blood cholesterol, lower blood pressure, improved self-esteem, and, possibly, stabilized body weight. You will no longer gain that one pound per year that so many people gain if you systematically train in the low heart zones, including Zone 1.

ALL ABOUT ZONE 2, THE GREEN ZONE

Training in Zone 2 increases skeletal muscle mass and decreases body fat. Oxygen is plentiful in this zone, so you realize improved aerobic function. In Zone 2, you expand your capacity to burn fat because you increase the number of energy factories, called *mitochondria*, in each muscle cell, and you metabolize fat more efficiently.

Zone 2, which is 60 to 70 percent of your maximum heart rate, or 70 to 80 percent of your threshold heart rate, is an ideal zone for warm-ups and cooldowns (or "warm-downs," as we like to call them) for most of your rides.

ALL ABOUT ZONE 3, THE YELLOW ZONE

Zone 3, the Aerobic Zone, which is 70 to 80 percent of your maximum heart rate or 80 to 90 percent of your threshold heart rate, gives you the biggest return on investment on your time in cycle training. In this zone, you maximize your efforts because you burn more calories than in Zone 2 and you burn a large amount of both carbohydrates and fat. Simultaneously, your body consumes lots of oxygen, and your cardiopulmonary system dramatically improves. Your maximum oxygen consumption (VO_2max) increases. Endorphins, the brain chemicals that blunt pain and are responsible for what is termed the "cyclist's high," are released. These naturally produced opiate-like stress reducers can increase up to fivefold from a resting state.

Zone 3 is the key fitness zone because you get fitter and faster when you train within it. During this training time, your body rids itself of stored-up emotional and physical toxins. You build resistance to fatigue and increase your endurance. Zone 3 riding builds cardiovascular efficiency while sparing the carbohydrates as you burn huge amounts of fat. The exercise high, or state of euphoria, arising from training here results in mood improvement, re-duced anxiety, and improved appetite control. Zone 3 leaves you feeling great for hours after the workout.

ALL ABOUT ZONE 4, THE ORANGE ZONE

When you cross into Zone 4, the Orange Zone, at 80 to 90 percent of your maximum heart rate, or 90 to 100 percent of your threshold heart rate, you enter a new territory of high heart rate numbers. Zone 4 leads to improved sports and fitness performance. If you want to get really fit, you must spend some riding time in this zone. If you are focused primarily on maintaining your current fitness level, you will spend little or no time in the Orange Zone.

Zone 4 is high-intensity training. It is much too stressful for the beginner, but for high-intensity workout junkies who spend a lot of their riding time hanging out in this zone, producing endorphins and eating up lactic acid as if it were chocolate, it is a delight. This is not an easy training zone to stay in because it is "hot": high heart rate numbers, high relative intensity, and high physical stresses. Being in Zone 4 is like riding in the blazing sun with no shade. Even exceedingly fit cyclists, elite-level riders, find it a challenge to stay above the midpoint of this zone for long.

ALL ABOUT ZONE 5, THE RED ZONE

You may have experienced Zone 5, the Red Zone, by accident if you ever had to sprint to catch the bus, when your heart was beating so hard and your breathing was so labored that you felt that your chest would burst. Red-lining, or riding in this 90 to 100 percent of your maximum heart rate zone or past your threshold heart rate, is riding in the zone above your lactate threshold or first ventilatory threshold. This is the territory where athletes suffer pain as they try to deliver the maximum energy to meet the metabolic demands of the highest-intensity training levels.

The Red Zone is not a sustainable training zone—your heart muscle cannot contract at or near its maximum intensity for long. For every second spent in this zone, you are taxing your oxygen capacity, fuels, heart, and skeletal muscles to their limits. Stay too long and you will reach complete exhaustion. The Red Zone tantalizes riders: You have to visit Zone 5 often enough to reach your highest performance levels, but if you overstay your visit (if you overtrain or overstrain), your body will not be very happy about letting you go back.

Table 5.2 summarizes everything you ever wanted to know about the Heart Zones.

HOW TO SET YOUR ZONES

In Chapter 4, you found either your maximum heart rate or your threshold heart rate and selected either the maximum heart rate program or the threshold heart rate program. Now you will learn how to set your heart zones for whichever program you selected. Remember, you do not need to use both programs, just one or the other. Selecting which program, maximum or threshold, is ultimately your decision. Read on to learn which is for you.

Setting Your Zones Based on Maximum Heart Rate

If you decided to anchor your zones on your maximum heart rate, you can use the value for your maximum heart rate that you determined in Chapter 4 using the Foster Talk Threshold Test. In addition, of the thirty rides included in Appendix A, there are three that you can use to verify and refine your measurement of maximum heart rate: Larger Than Life, Hill Sprints, and The All-Out Trip. We recommend that you remeasure your maximum heart rate periodically, using the submax test, to make sure that you are working with an accurate value.

If you take a look at the full-color insert in this chapter, you will find the Maximum Heart Rate chart. First, locate the number in the top row that corresponds most closely with your estimated maximum heart rate, and then record

TABLE 5.2 All About the Heart Zones

Zone	Fuel Burned (per minute)	Calories Burned (Cal/min) (Cal/30ml)	Ride Objective	Benefits	HZT Points	Wellness Zones	Intensity Measurements				
							Lactate Concentration	VO_2	Rating of Perceived Exertion	Description of Perceived Exertion	Talk
1 50%–60% max 60%–79% threshold	10% carbohydrate, 85% fat, 5% protein	<4 cal/min <120	Warm-up and cool-down; rehabilitation	Improved self-esteem, stress reduction, blood chemistry, improved fitness	x1	Health	<2 mmol/L	28–39	1–2	Easy to very easy	Easy conversation, just like sitting and talking
2 60%–70% max 70%–80% threshold	15% carbohydrate, 80% fat, 5% protein	<7 cal/min <210	Recovery, regeneration, and aerobic endurance	Improved fat mobilization, basic cardio training; staying fit	x2	Health to Fitness	2–3 mmol/L	40–58	2–4	Easy to somewhat hard	Aware of breathing, very comfortable talking
3 70%–80% max 80%–90% threshold	55% carbohydrate, 40% fat, 5% protein	<10 cal/min <300	Tempo, muscular strength, and endurance	Improved aerobic capacity, optimal cardiovascular at training; becoming fitter	x3	Fitness	3–4 mmol/L	49–70	4–6	Hard to somewhat hard	Very aware of breathing, still comfortable to talk
4 80%–90% max 90%–100% threshold	70% carbohydrate, 25% fat, 5% protein	<15 cal/min <450	Time trial intervals, tempo, hill work	Improved anaerobic capacity, lactate clearance	x4	Performance	4–8 mmol/L	71–83	6–8	Very hard to very, very hard	Can still talk, but not comfortably VT_1 = 80% max heart rate
5 90%–100% max 100+% threshold (a, b, and c)	90% carbohydrate, 5% fat, 5% protein	<20 cal/min <600	Max effort, speed, and power	Improved lactate tolerance, VO_2, and nonaerobic power	x5	Performance	>8 mmol/L	84–100	8–10	Maximal effort to very, very hard	Can't talk except for very short phrases VT_2 = 90% max heart rate

TABLE 5.3 Recording Your Maximum Heart Rate Zones		
Maximum Heart Rate Zones	Floor (bpm)	Ceiling (bpm)
Zone 5		
Zone 4		
Zone 3		
Zone 2		
Zone 1		

that number. Next, notice that the column below your maximum heart rate is divided into zones. The top number in each of the zones is called the *ceiling*, and the bottom number is called the *floor*. You can see that the number at the top of each zone is the same number as the bottom of the zone above it. Write down the ceiling and floor of each of your cycling heart zones in Table 5.3.

The first thing you will want to do is memorize the top and the bottom of Zone 3, the Aerobic Zone. This is a shorthand way to remember quickly where you are in the five zones: Everything above these numbers is Zone 4 or Zone 5, and everything below them is Zone 2 or Zone 1.

You have now set your five zones based on maximum heart rate. These zones are static—they do not change. The "weight" of the zones increases in a linear fashion. In other words, the amount of exertion you are experiencing in Zone 2 is two times as much as the exertion in Zone 1; exertion in Zone 3 is three times as much as in Zone 1; and so on. As you get fitter, your zones stay the same. Remember, though, that the anchor point, maximum heart rate, is sport-specific. If you are training in more than one sport (more than one modality), then you have to determine your maximum heart rate and set your zones for each sport, and for each mode of activity.

Setting Your Zones Based on Threshold Heart Rate

If you decided to anchor your zones on your threshold heart rate, you can use the value for threshold heart rate that you determined in Chapter 4 using the Foster Talk Threshold Test. Appendix A also includes two rides that you can use to verify and refine your measurement of threshold heart rate: Threshold Endurance Road Test and the Threshold Road Cycling Test. We recommend that you remeasure your threshold heart rate monthly because your threshold increases as you become more fit.

To set your zones anchored on threshold heart rate, refer again to the full-color insert in this chapter, but this time to the Threshold Heart Rate Zones chart.

Find the "Threshold" row. Reading left to right, find the number that most closely corresponds to your estimated threshold heart rate. Write down that number. Next, note that the zones below your threshold heart rate are numbered 1, 2, 3, and 4. Then, notice the zones above your threshold heart rate: 5a, 5b, and 5c.

Looking at the chart, you can see that each column is divided into zones. The top number in each of the zones is called the *ceiling*, and the bottom number is called the *floor*. Record the ceiling and the floor of each of your cycling threshold heart zones in Table 5.4.

As you learned in Chapter 4, the different exertion levels required in each zone can also be gauged by your ventilatory or breathing response, or by perceived exertion.

Comparing the Zones

The difference between the zones based on maximum heart rate and threshold heart rate rises above Zone 4. With maximum heart rate, Zone 5 is one continuous zone stretching from 90 percent to 100 percent of maximum heart rate, whereas with threshold heart rate, Zone 5 is subdivided into three parts: 5a, 5b,

TABLE 5.4 Recording Your Threshold Heart Rate Zones		
Threshold Heart Rate Zones	Floor (bpm)	Ceiling (bpm)
Zone 5c		
Zone 5b		
Zone 5a		
Threshold		
Zone 4		
Zone 3		
Zone 2		
Zone 1		

and 5c. This subdivision of Zone 5 emphasizes the exponential increases in physiological cost as you climb up the curve past your threshold heart rate. Table 5.5 compares maximum heart zones with threshold heart rate zones.

Each of the heart zones has its own unique ride types and intensity levels. As you go higher in the zones, the duration of the rides necessarily decreases. As you ride into the higher zones, the perceived effort increases. Table 5.6 describes what riding tactics are common to each of the zones and how you might go about working them into your training.

MULTIPLE ZONES GIVE MULTIPLE BENEFITS

Each of the heart zones is part of the wellness continuum from health (Zones 1 through 3) to fitness (Zones 2 through 4) to performance (Zones 3 through 5).

TABLE 5.5 Comparing Maximum Heart Rate Zones and Threshold Heart Rate Zones

Threshold Heart Rate Zones	Percentage of Threshold Heart Rate (HR)	Maximum Heart Rate Zones	Percentage of Maximum Heart Rate	Breathing Effort	Respiratory Rate	Training Benefit	Rating of Perceived Exertion
5c	Max HR–110%			Cannot talk, ready to stop	Unsustainable for long	Maximizing sprint power	10
5b	109%–105%			Very rapid breathing and very uncomfortable; don't want to talk	Very, very fast	Maximize power	8.5–9
5a	104%–100%	5	100%–91%	Challenging, deep, and rapid breathing; don't talk unless have to	Fast	Improve max VO_2	7–8.5
4	100%–91%	4	90%–81%	Not sure if speaking is comfortable (VT_1), on the verge of not being able to talk	Rapid	Improved aerobic capacity and lactic acid tolerance	6–7
3	90%–81%	3	80%–71%	More difficult to talk; becoming uncomfortable	Moderate	Aerobic endurance	4–6
2	80%–71%	2	70%–61%	Can talk without interruption or difficulty	Easy	Improved aerobic function	2–4
1	70%–61%	1	60%–51%	Comfortable and easy breathing	Low	Recuperative, warm-up and cool-down	1–2

TABLE 5.6 **Overview of Riding in the Threshold Heart Rate Zones**

Threshold Heart Rate Zones	Duration	Training Objective	Riding Suggestions
5c	10- to 45-second intervals not to exceed 5 to 10 minutes	Increase your power, speed, and nonaerobic (nonoxidative) capacity.	Short hill repeats; sprint intervals. Recommend near-complete rest between intervals. Explosive jumps.
5b	1- to 4-minute intervals not to exceed 10–12 minutes	Improve your VO$_2$max. Adaptations include improved tolerance to lactate levels and increase in cardiac function, primarily stroke volume.	Intervals: 3 × 2 minutes at VO$_2$max or 3–5 hill repeats 3–5 minutes rest between intervals.
5a	3- to 15-minute intervals not to exceed 20–60 minutes	Raise your threshold heart rate, power, speed, and percentage of VO$_2$max. Improve your lactate tolerance.	Interval training: Three times three miles above threshold; recover down to 60% maximum heart rate up to 5 minutes; repeat.
4	10–90 minutes	Improve your ability to ride fast for long periods to sustain power output, which results in improved competitions.	High-intensity steady state rides or long intervals for 5–20 minutes. Rides at just below your 40K time trial pace.
3	1–3 hours	Improve your ability to deliver more oxygen to the working muscles, and improve their ability to use oxygen in muscular work.	Tempo riding on rolling terrain with moderate climbing; training adaptations include increase in capillarization, number of mitochondria, and amount of aerobic enzymes.
2	2–6 hours	Improve your aerobic base and your fatigue resistance.	Weekly "long" rides at the beginning of the season; base training. You can talk easily and continuously at this effort level.
1	20–60 minutes	This is the warm-up and cool-down zone, and a place to spend time if you are recovering from previous hard efforts.	Easy 30-minute spin to keep the muscles active and the heart rate low. Good way to spend the day after a race or hard ride day.

HEART ZONES TRAINING

MAXIMUM HEART RATE

HEART ZONES TRAINING

Training Zone (% maximum heart rate)	Fuel Burned*	Max HR 160	Max HR 165	Max HR 170	Max HR 175	Max HR 180	Max HR 185	Max HR 190	Max HR 195	Max HR 200	Max HR 205	Max HR 210	Max HR 215	Max HR 220	Max HR 225	Max HR 230	Max HR 235	Max HR 240
Z5 RED LINE 90%-100%		160 ◆ 144	165 ◆ 149	170 ◆ 153	175 ◆ 158	180 ◆ 162	185 ◆ 167	190 ◆ 171	195 ◆ 176	200 ◆ 180	205 ◆ 185	210 ◆ 189	215 ◆ 194	220 ◆ 198	225 ◆ 203	230 ◆ 207	235 ◆ 211	240 ◆ 216
Z4 THRESHOLD 80%-90%		144 ◆ 128	149 ◆ 132	153 ◆ 136	158 ◆ 140	162 ◆ 144	167 ◆ 148	171 ◆ 152	176 ◆ 156	180 ◆ 160	185 ◆ 164	189 ◆ 168	194 ◆ 172	198 ◆ 176	203 ◆ 180	207 ◆ 184	211 ◆ 188	216 ◆ 192
Z3 AEROBIC 70%-80%		128 ◆ 112	132 ◆ 116	136 ◆ 119	140 ◆ 123	144 ◆ 126	148 ◆ 130	152 ◆ 133	156 ◆ 137	160 ◆ 140	164 ◆ 143	168 ◆ 147	172 ◆ 151	176 ◆ 154	180 ◆ 158	184 ◆ 164	188 ◆ 165	192 ◆ 168
Z2 TEMPERATE 60%-70%		112 ◆ 96	116 ◆ 99	119 ◆ 102	123 ◆ 105	126 ◆ 108	130 ◆ 111	133 ◆ 114	137 ◆ 117	140 ◆ 120	143 ◆ 123	147 ◆ 126	151 ◆ 129	154 ◆ 132	158 ◆ 135	164 ◆ 138	165 ◆ 141	168 ◆ 144
Z1 HEALTHY HEART 50%-60%		96 ◆ 80	99 ◆ 83	102 ◆ 85	105 ◆ 88	108 ◆ 90	111 ◆ 93	114 ◆ 95	117 ◆ 98	120 ◆ 100	123 ◆ 103	126 ◆ 105	129 ◆ 108	132 ◆ 110	135 ◆ 113	138 ◆ 115	141 ◆ 118	144 ◆ 120

* amount of fat burned
* amount of carbohydrates burned

© Copyright 2005 by Heart Zones Company, 2636 Fulton Avenue, Suite 100, Sacramento, CA 95821
Phone: 916.481.7283 • Fax: 916.481.2213 • Email: info@heartzones.com • Website: www.heartzones.com

5 STEPS TO BETTER FITNESS AND PERFORMANCE

1. **Choose your Heart Zone:** Select one of the five different training zones based on the exercise goals for your workout.
2. **Set your Maximum Heart Rate:** Find your maximum heart rate (Max HR) along the top horizontal row of numbers.
3. **Determine your Training Zone:** The box where your selected training zone and Max HR column intersect is your heart rate training zone.
4. **Set the Zone:** The lower heart rate number in this box is the floor of your training zone and the upper number is the ceiling.
5. **Stay in Zone:** During each workout, maintain your heart rate between your zone floor and ceiling (excluding warm up and cool down).

HEART ZONES®
TRAINING AND EDUCATION COMPANY

THRESHOLD HEART RATE CHART ©

TRAINING ZONE	NAME	INTENSITY	PERCENT	BEATS PER MINUTE																	
Zone 5c	RED	NON AEROBIC	>110%	132	138	143	149	154	160	165	171	176	182	187	193	198	204	209	215	220
Zone 5b	RED	NON AEROBIC	105%↔110%	126↔132	131↔138	137↔143	142↔149	147↔154	152↔160	158↔165	163↔171	168↔176	173↔182	178↔187	184↔193	189↔198	194↔204	200↔209	205↔215	210↔220
Zone 5a		NON AEROBIC	100%↔105%	120↔126	125↔131	130↔137	135↔142	140↔147	145↔152	150↔158	155↔163	160↔168	165↔173	170↔178	175↔184	180↔189	185↔194	190↔200	195↔205	200↔210
ANCHOR POINT		THRESHOLD	100%	120	125	130	135	140	145	150	155	160	165	170	175	180	185	190	195	200
Zone 4	ORANGE		90%↔100%	108↔120	113↔125	117↔130	122↔135	126↔140	130↔145	135↔150	140↔155	144↔160	149↔165	153↔170	158↔175	162↔180	167↔185	171↔190	176↔195	180↔200
Zone 3	YELLOW	AEROBIC	80%↔90%	96↔108	100↔113	104↔117	108↔122	112↔126	116↔130	120↔135	124↔140	128↔144	132↔149	136↔153	140↔158	144↔162	148↔167	152↔171	156↔176	160↔180
Zone 2	GREEN		70%↔80%	84↔96	88↔100	91↔104	95↔108	98↔112	102↔116	105↔120	109↔124	112↔128	115↔132	119↔136	123↔140	126↔144	130↔148	133↔152	137↔156	140↔160
Zone 1	BLUE		60%↔70%	72↔84	75↔88	78↔91	81↔95	84↔98	87↔102	90↔105	93↔109	96↔112	99↔115	102↔119	105↔123	108↔126	111↔130	114↔133	117↔137	120↔140

Heart Zones USA ◆ 2636 Fulton Avenue Suite 100 ◆ Sacramento, California 95821 ◆ USA ◆ 916-481-7283 ◆ www.heartzones.com ◆ Copyright 2005

If you want to concentrate on health benefits, you train in the health zones, the low zones. If you want fitness benefits, you train in the fitness zones, the zones in the middle. For performance outcomes, you spend time in the high zones of 3, 4, and 5. If you want all of these benefits, you must train in all the zones. Training in one zone gives you the benefits from only that one zone. The more you train in different zones, the more you get all of the different benefits.

Though it might be wonderful if training benefits were cumulative, allowing you to reap the benefits of Zones 1 and 2 from training in Zone 3, that is not the way human physiology works. Each zone features its own unique, specific metabolic and exercise stress characteristics. You need to spend the majority of your time in the lower zones. In fact, spending too much time in the higher zones can actually be detrimental to your health.

However, each day you certainly can train in more than one zone and derive all the wellness benefits that way. On one day, cycle in Zone 1 and Zone 2, and use this as an active recovery day—a fun, low-intensity, emotionally easy ride day. The next day, ride in and out of Zone 5 with high-intensity intervals to train your physiology to its highest ability. The following day, train in Zone 2, effortlessly enjoying the "no pain, lots of gain" road to positive results. Then train in Zone 3, the Aerobic Zone, multiplying your mitochondrial density so you can burn more fat and do it more efficiently. Take the next day off for a 100 percent full rest day for total recovery. Try some crosstraining, too, which pays off by improving your cardiovascular capacity without taxing your sport-specific muscles.

TRAINING IN ZONES IS STATE OF THE ART

You already know that the Heart Zones Training methodology uses zones, setting goals, connecting you with your heart through the use of tools, and anchoring the program with a particular heart rate so that you can establish heart rate zones. The two most common anchor points in this methodology are maximum heart rate and threshold heart rate. We thought you might like to know that several other training methodologies also rest on a foundation similar to Heart Zones. Carl Foster, PhD, current president of the American College of Sports Medicine, says the following:

> There are three contemporary scientists/coaches who have centered their training and methodology based on something analogous to the Heart Zones. The VDOT approach of Jack Daniels, PhD, a highly regarded running coach and exercise physiologist based at the University of Northern Arizona; the polarized model of Stephen Seiler, PhD, exercise physiologist at Agdar College in Norway; and the VO_2max approach of Veronique Billat, PhD, at the University of Evry, outside of Paris, all use a zone-based approach to training.

Daniels Training System

Jack Daniels, PhD, coach and author of *Daniels' Running Formula* (*Runner's World* called him the World's Greatest Track Coach in the late 1990s), uses a four-zone model based on percentage of VO_2max. His training zones are really speed zones because they are based on running speed and not heart rate per se. Table 5.7 shows how Daniels's system corresponds to Heart Zones.

Daniels's general mixture is 70 percent or more easy running, with the other types of training mixed in for effect. He uses a rotating periodization

TABLE 5.7 Comparison of Pace: Daniels Training System and the Heart Zones

Pace (Daniels)	Equivalent Threshold Heart Zones
Easy running	Zones 1, 2, and 3
Threshold runs	Transition between Zones 4 and 5
vVO_2max runs	Top of Zone 5 or Zone 5c
Repetition runs	Above Zone 5 (5a, 5b, 5c)

scheme but basically recommends three hard days one week (two of them together) and two hard days the next week. The hard days rotate among threshold runs, vVO$_2$max runs (vVO$_2$ is velocity at your maximum aerobic capacity or VO$_2$), and repetition runs at particular parts of the season.

Daniels's approach is remarkable in that many of his athletes complain that they are training too easily, but they cannot complain about the results. After all, he has coached Olympic medalists and championship college athletes who were not expected to be standing on the victory platform.

Seiler Training System

Stephen Seiler is the author of the polarized model. His work, largely with elite rowers and elite junior cross-country skiers, suggests that the majority of training should be done at relatively low intensity (comparable to Heart Zones 1 through 3) but that a critical 10 to 15 percent of training should be done at high intensity (i.e., Zone 5). In the Seiler system, training in what is equivalent to Zone 4 (which Dr. Foster calls "the black hole") occurs primarily in the transition from low- to high-intensity training.

Seiler notes that progression from year to year in an athlete's career is largely based on maintaining this general formula, with progressive increases in total training load. He even suggests that in order to do the high-intensity training that is critical for improved racing success, the athlete has to do more and more background training.

Seiler's research has been supported by findings from the work of Alejandro Lucia, MD, PhD, as well as by Dr. Foster. Briefly stated, at least 70 percent of training should occur at lower intensity (Zones 1 through 3), 10 percent should be more or less equivalent to Zone 4, and 10 percent to 20 percent should be equivalent to Zone 5. Work from Dr. Lucia's graduate student Jonathan Esteve-Llano suggests that taking time out of Zone 4 and adding it to Zones 1, 2, and 3 is profitable. Most likely, about 10 percent of training must be done in Zone 5.

Billat Training System

The approach of French researcher Veronique Billat, PhD, is similar in many ways to that of Jack Daniels, in that she recommends vVO_2max and threshold runs two to three days per week. In contrast to Daniels, however, she recommends that the duration of the vVO_2max runs be 50 percent of the time that vVO_2max can be sustained. Ideally, this is determined in the laboratory, but one can use an estimate of six minutes as what Billat calls the "time limit at vVO_2max," meaning you do repeat three-minute runs at a pace you can sustain for six minutes (interpolated from prior racing performances). Billat has evidence that vVO_2max runs may contribute to improving efficiency, which is clearly the way for athletes with already well-developed "motors" to improve.

Like Daniels, Billat argues that two to three days per week of high-intensity training (in Zones 4 and 5) is all that may be profitably tolerated.

THE IMPORTANCE OF INDIVIDUALITY

Clearly, there is no one right way to train. Training is individual. Your response to the training stimulus is different from that of other athletes; each person can handle different amounts, frequencies, and types of training stresses. The real issue is not which training system is best for your riding performances, but rather how you apply a system to your unique training capacity. That brings us to periodization and training load, coming up in the next chapter.

PERIODIZE YOUR TRAINING LOAD

THE UPS AND DOWNS OF PERIODIZATION

Periodization is all about taking your training intensity level up and down, over and over, over the course of your training plan. In other words, it is designing a training plan that introduces variation in your training load (more on that later) over time. It is the exact opposite of those early "no pain, no gain" workouts that sought to keep you at the highest intensity possible for as long as possible as often as possible. We are done with that!

Periodization Brings Variation to Your Training

You may recall that the second principle of Heart Zones Training is "Multiple heart zones lead to multiple benefits." Periodization is how you ensure that you train in multiple heart zones over the course of each workout and over the course of your entire training plan. It does not matter whether you are anchoring zones on maximum heart rate or on threshold heart rate; the process of periodizing your training is the same either way.

Periodizing your training plan means dividing up your long-term training program into discrete blocks of time and varying both training intensity and skill set from one block to the next and within the blocks. Working at different levels of intensity over time improves your overall fitness, teaches you to cope with fatigue both physically and mentally, makes training more enjoyable, lowers your risk of injury, and helps you avoid the dangers of overtraining.

Periodization introduces structure and efficiency to your training plan, allowing you to make the most of each ride or workout session. You do not waste time on rides that do not help you reach your goal—better performance on event day.

PERIODIZATION IS . . .

- the distribution and sequencing of training load over time.
- a way of organizing training into three cycles: macrocycle, mesocycle, and microcycle.
- the application of different amounts of training load at different periods of time.
- changing the weekly, monthly, seasonal, and yearly ride schedule.
- making sure that this year's riding is different from last year's.
- stress followed by strain followed by rest that leads to adaptation.
- a way to build a training plan with structure and discipline.

Tweaking Training Load

Periodization is the scheduling and forecasting of training by varying *training load* over discrete periods of time. We are not actually going to get into the details of training load until later in the chapter, but it suffices to say for now that training load is a measure of the volume of work being done. It is a multidimensional way to look at effort or exertion that takes into account intensity (as measured by heart rate) and time.

You do not have to get out your calculator in order to understand periodization on a fundamental, intuitive level. Just imagine that you ride hard

TABLE 6.1	Six Principles of Periodization
PERSONALIZATION	There is no one correct way to periodize training; personalize your periodization.
VARIABILITY	To prevent training monotony and to stimulate the training effect, vary your workouts by type of ride and by type of intensity.
PLANNING	Build the plan by scheduling rides that focus on each aspect of riding: tactical, emotional, technical, and physical.
TIME	Determine the amount of time you realistically have for training, and use that time efficiently.
RECORD KEEPING	Accurate logging is critical to gauging the effectiveness of a training program. Record details about the training and about the context (your life) in which the training occurs—injuries, distractions, nutrition, and emotions.
RECOVERY	Rest when the schedule calls for rest, and work when it calls for work.

for a while, then back off a bit, then ride really hard for a few minutes, and then go easy. You can imagine what a graph of your effort over time would look like: a hill, then flat, a bigger hill, and then flat again. That is periodization in a nutshell. As you might imagine, however, the inside of the nut can get complicated, and that is what we explore next.

Principles of Periodization

At Heart Zones, we like principles. They serve as valuable reference points and keep us on track. Table 6.1 lists six principles of periodization.

Macro, Meso, and Micro: The Building Blocks

A periodized training plan is defined by three kinds of time intervals: one macrocycle, a few mesocycles, and several microcycles. The macrocycle (*macro*—large) is the biggest increment of time in your training plan, lasting from several months to one year in length. A mesocycle (*meso*—middle) is

TABLE 6.2 Comparing Macro-, Meso-, and Microcycles

Time Increment	Duration	Description
MACROCYCLE	Several months to one year	One complete training cycle from start to finish, consisting of several mesocycles
MESOCYCLE	Several weeks to several months	Intermediate phase in which the rider focuses on creating a defined adaptation or skill outcome. The mesocycles focus on preparation, competition, and transition.
MICROCYCLE	Seven to fourteen days	A short period with specific developmental objectives

the intermediate increment of time between the largest and the smallest; there are several mesocycles in a macrocycle, and each mesocycle lasts anywhere from several weeks to several months. Last, a microcycle (*micro*—small) is the smallest increment of time in the training plan, usually lasting from seven to fourteen days. As you might imagine, two or more microcycles make up a mesocycle.

Wondering where actual ride sessions fit into this scheme? Think of each workout session as a basic building block of the training plan; several workout sessions occur in each microcycle. Table 6.2 shows how these time intervals compare.

Different Mesocycles for Different Purposes

With Heart Zones Cycling training plans, three types of mesocycles comprise the macrocycle: the preparation mesocycle(s), the competition mesocycle(s), and the transition mesocycle. Some coaches refer to these three categories as "blocks":

Preparation block(s). One or more foundation periods that includes both general and specific training.

Competition block. The training period during the competitive season.

Transition block. The training period during the off-season that allows for physical and emotional regeneration of the rider.

Blocks can be made up of one or more mesocycles. For example, your preparation block will probably include mesocycles focusing on your base fitness, endurance, strength, and power. Each of those mesocycles in turn might be made up of several microcycles that each has an even more narrowly defined focus. Blocks can last for several weeks or several months, depending on the category of the rider and the focus of the training. These definitions of blocks and mesocycles are flexible, so the specific vocabulary is not that important; the important thing is the concept that in periodization, you break your training into discrete segments of time, each with a different training focus.

PERIODIZATION MEANS PLANNING YOUR TRAINING TIME

Periodization is the organizing principle behind your training plan. It provides structure to your training schedule and to your selection of particular rides on particular days. Thus, the first element in periodization is time. Working with the time elements of periodization involves five basic steps:

STEP 1. Put your goal event on the calendar, and work backward from that date.

STEP 2. Determine the length of your macrocycle in weeks.

STEP 3. Divide your macrocycle into blocks or mesocycles.

STEP 4. Divide your mesocycles into microcycles.

STEP 5. Plug workout details into your microcycles.

We will focus for now on steps 1 through 3; steps 4 and 5 are discussed a little later in this chapter.

First, get a calendar and write down the date of the event for which you are training. This will give you a concrete goal to work toward, which is crucial to your success. If you are a high achiever and have more than one big event to train for, excellent! Put *all* your events on the calendar! For step 2, determine how many weeks there are between the date on which your training begins and your goal event. This is the length of your macrocycle.

Completing step 3 involves understanding that a macrocycle is divided into four distinct periods of time in which to focus on different aspects of your training:

- Preparation 1
- Preparation 2
- Event or Competition Training
- Transition

Each of these time periods consists of one or more mesocycles. Preparation 1 is devoted to general conditioning (building your base) and endurance. Preparation 2 begins your event-specific training and continues to build endurance, power, and strength; this is the mesocycle in which your training hits its highest-intensity level. Event or Competition Training is the mesocycle in which you focus on event-specific skills while building toward peak performance. Transition, the shortest of the mesocycles, is devoted to regeneration, both mentally and physically.

Figure 6.1 provides a rudimentary outline of a macrocycle, mesocycle, and microcycle.

BEGIN TO FOCUS ON THE DETAILS

Constructing a detailed periodized training plan involves determining how to distribute intensity and skill development over the course of each mesocycle, each microcycle, each week, and each ride.

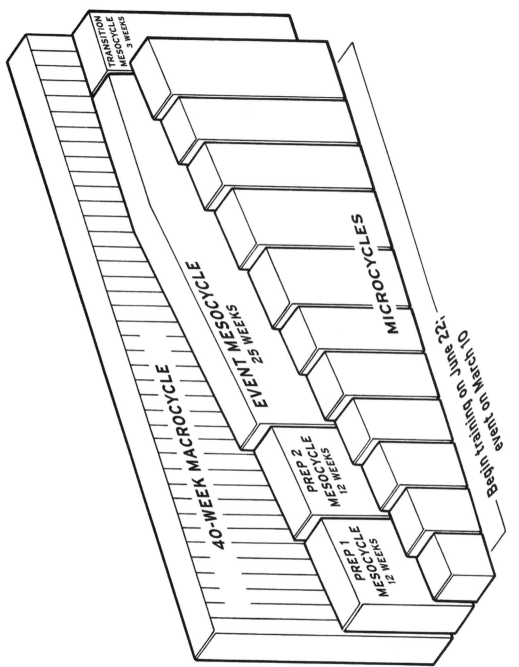

FIGURE 6.1 Outline of a 40-Week Macrocycle

TABLE 6.3 A Guide to the Mesocycles				
Factor	Preparation 1	Preparation 2	Event/Competition	Transition
OVERALL PURPOSE	Establishing base level of endurance	Improving base, strength, speed, and power while focusing on specific event requirements	Training to reach optimum performance capacity	Reducing training to allow for the regeneration process to occur
INTENSITY	Maximum Heart Rate Zones 2–3; Threshold Heart Rate Zones 2–3	Maximum Heart Rate Zones 3–5; Threshold Heart Rate Zones 3–5	Maximum Heart Rate Zones 3–5; Threshold Heart Rate Zones 3–5+	Maximum Heart Rate Zones 1–3; Threshold Heart Rate Zones 1–3
ENERGY SYSTEMS	Aerobic to threshold	Aerobic to nonaerobic	All	Low to moderate aerobic
TIME AND MILEAGE	Moderate to high	Moderate to high; then back to moderate at the end	Moderate	Low
LOAD	Increases progressively from low to moderate	Moderate to high; then back to moderate	Moderate	Low
SKILLS	General riding skills and techniques	Event-specific skills and techniques	Racing or event-specific skills (e.g., time trials, attacks, climbing, sprinting, etc.)	Ride for enjoyment
WEIGHT TRAINING AND CROSSTRAINING	Yes	Yes, but diminishing	Little, possibly none	Yes

The six principles of periodization give you the "big picture"—the theoretical underpinnings of a periodized training plan. The "midrange" details come from the combination of the various factors that determine the nature of each mesocycle. Table 6.3 provides you with an overview of each type of mesocycle.

HOW TO DISTRIBUTE INTENSITY: THE TRAINING TREE

The fundamental issue in both your short-term and long-term planning is how to distribute training intensity and load over time. In the Heart Zones

Training methodology, intensity is represented by heart zones. Therefore, distributing variable degrees of training intensity over the course of your training plan (your macrocycle) involves manipulating the amount of time that you spend in each heart zone. If you are anchoring your training program using maximum heart rate, you will distribute your available training time among Zones 1 through 5. If you are anchoring your training program using threshold heart rate, you will distribute your available training time among Zones 1 through 5c. Notice we did not say "distribute your time *equally*." The distribution of time in each zone varies according to the focus of the particular mesocycle.

We have developed a model for distributing time in each zone called the Training Tree (see Figure 6.2).

The tree represents the idea that your training is built on a sturdy foundation (i.e., the trunk), and each limb or branch of the tree develops the fitness you need to become a well-rounded cyclist. Table 6.4 gives an overview of each branch of the Training Tree.

Each limb on the Training Tree represents a different mesocycle. As you gain the fitness or the skills from one limb, then it is time to climb up to the next mesocycle, or the next limb. You will see that as you climb from one mesocycle to the next, you increase training load by training progressively in higher heart zones that have higher values. Both in planning and in training, you will begin to see how each limb or mesocycle of the tree builds on the preceding one.

The Training Tree's Sturdy "Trunk"

Look at the bottom of a Training Tree, where you will find the Transition mesocycle. Transition is the period of time between the Competition mesocycle and Preparation 1, or the beginning of the next season. After a season of reaching new fitness levels on the bike, finishing the big events, and racing better than ever before, all riders need a period for regeneration. This is a time

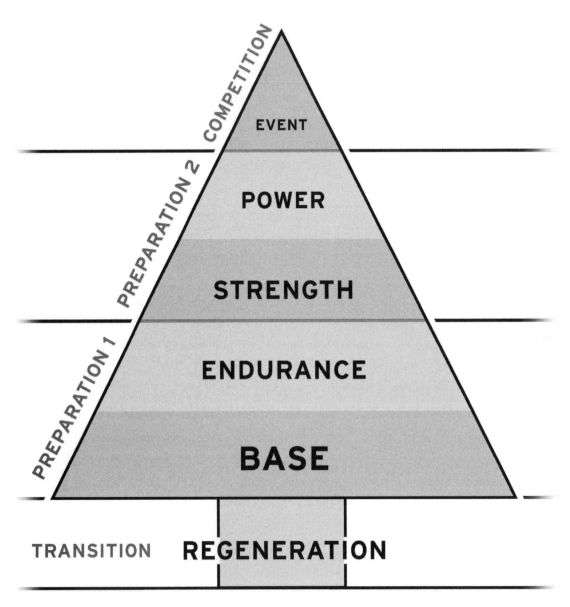

FIGURE 6.2 Heart Zones Cycling Training Tree

TABLE 6.4 Branches of the Training Tree for Threshold (T) and Maximum (M) Heart Rate

Branch	Mesocycle	Purpose	Physiological Adaptation	Zone	Terrain
EVENT	Competition	Training to reach optimal performance capacity; putting it all together to ride faster and longer	Increased aerobic and nonaerobic capacity; peak readiness	T: z2–5c M: z2–5	Varied
POWER	Prep 2	Improving power while focusing on specific event requirements	Increased aerobic and nonaerobic capacity	T: z2–5c M: z2–5	Varied
STRENGTH	Prep 2	Building volume and intensity with a focus on hills and threshold improvement	Increased aerobic capacity, muscular strength, and endurance	T: z2–5 M: z2–4	Varied
ENDURANCE	Prep 1	Building volume and intensity	Increased aerobic capacity and muscular endurance	z1–3	Flat to hills
BASE	Prep 1	As starting point for training program, gradually building volume or time in the saddle at a low intensity	Aerobic endurance and development of cycling-specific muscles	z1–2	Flat to rolling hills
REGENERATION	Transition	A time for regeneration and recovery; goal setting for next season	Physical, mental, and emotional recuperation	z1–2	Cross-training

for emotional recuperation, for physical rest to allow depleted energy stores and stressed neuromuscular tissues to recover, and for social activities and spending time with your family and friends. Most of all, the transition mesocycle is a period to reflect on the season, renew your commitment to training, set new goals, and return to the heart of riding.

The Training Tree as a Guideline for "Time in Zone"

The Training Tree varies the time you spend in each zone to distribute the intensity of the rides over the course of a given mesocycle. Notice that Table 6.5 describes volume or time in percentages rather than minutes. These are percentages of your available training time, allowing you to adapt the Training Tree to your personal schedule. For example, if you have 10 hours (600 minutes) to train over two weeks, and the Training Tree specifies that you should spend 40 percent of that time in Zone 3, then you will plan rides that give you 240 minutes (40 percent of 600 minutes) in Zone 3 over the course of the two weeks.

Let's focus for a moment on the Endurance branch of the Training Tree:

Assume that for the first week of this mesocycle, you have determined that you have a time budget of 8 hours (480 minutes) to ride. Your training time will be distributed among the zones like this: 96 minutes in Zone 1, 144 minutes in Zone 2, 192 minutes in Zone 3, and 48 minutes in Zone 4.

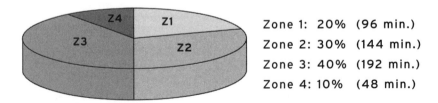

Zone 1: 20% (96 min.)
Zone 2: 30% (144 min.)
Zone 3: 40% (192 min.)
Zone 4: 10% (48 min.)

FIGURE 6.3   Endurance Branch: Calculating Your Training Time

There are two different Training Trees, one for zones anchored on maximum heart rate (see Table 6.5) and another for zones anchored on threshold heart rate (see Table 6.6).

The two Training Trees are nearly identical until you reach Zone 5 in any given branch. With maximum heart rate, Zone 5 represents from 90 to 100 percent of maximum heart rate, whereas with threshold heart rate, Zone 5 is divided into three subzones: 5a is 100 to 105 percent above threshold, 5b is 105 to 110 percent of threshold, and 5c is above 110 percent of threshold.

TABLE 6.5   Heart Zones Training Tree for Maximum Heart Rate

		Zones				
		1	2	3	4	5
Mesocycle	*Branch*	Aerobic				Non-aerobic
COMPETITION		10%	20%	30%	35%	5%
PREPARATION 2: Event-Specific Training	Power	—	5%	30%	40%	25%
	Strength	10%	10%	30%	50%	—
PREPARATION 1: Conditioning and Technique	Endurance	20%	30%	40%	10%	—
	Base	20%	40%	30%	10%	—
TRANSITION		10%	20%	60%	10%	—

TABLE 6.6   Heart Zones Training Tree for Threshold Heart Rate

		Zones							
		1	2	3	4		5a	5b	5c
Mesocycle	*Branch*	Aerobic				Threshold	Nonaerobic		
COMPETITION		10%	20%	30%	35%	—	3%	1%	1%
PREPARATION 2: Event-Specific Training	Power	—	5%	30%	40%	—	15%	7%	3%
	Strength	10%	10%	30%	50%	—	—	—	—
PREPARATION 1: Conditioning and Technique	Endurance	20%	30%	40%	10%	—	—	—	—
	Base	20%	40%	30%	10%	—	—	—	—
TRANSITION		10%	20%	60%	10%	—	—	—	—

Rules of the Training Tree

The Training Tree provides a powerful blueprint for organizing and distributing your training intensity over the course of your macrocycle. As you begin to ponder the Training Tree, keep these rules in mind:

RULE 1. The bigger the base, the higher the peak. All riders will spend the greatest percentage of their time in Preparation 1 building their base. The main focus must be general conditioning. Small amounts of higher-intensity training can be included during this training period to maintain neuromuscular coordination.

RULE 2. Specific events require specific training. During the strength branch in the Preparation 2 mesocycle, it is critical to train to the specific needs demanded for the specific events you will be entering.

RULE 3. Decrease load to peak. Just prior to the event, decrease your overall training volume, but maintain similar intensity levels. In other words, train intensely, but for shorter amounts of time.

FILLING IN THE BLANKS: MICROCYCLES

Now that you know how mesocycles work, it is time to look at microcycles. A microcycle is the set of individual rides and workouts over a period of seven to fourteen days. A microcycle may include single or double workout days. The heart of periodization is the process of manipulating microcycles to create variability in your training plan. Within each microcycle, your body should undergo varying degrees of volume and intensity followed by rest. As your body responds to this cyclical sequence, it adapts physiologically. This results in the training effect that leads to better performance. One very good way to organize your thinking about how to distribute training intensity over the course of each microcycle is to think in terms of training load, which is explained in the next section.

TRAINING LOAD = TRAINING "WORK"

Training load is the summation of the amount of stress that you experience over a period of time; it is a measure of the amount of "work" you do during your training.

TABLE 6.7 Zone Weight: Intensity Values for Heart Zones

Max Zone	Threshold Zone	=	Zone Weight (Intensity)
1	1		1
2	2		2
3	3		3
4	4		4
5	T		5
—	5a		6
—	5b		7
—	5c		8

Calculating Training Load

Two factors go into measuring training load: intensity and volume. Intensity is represented by heart zones, and volume is measured by the time (minutes) spent in a given zone. To calculate intensity, each of the heart zones is given a numerical value; the higher the zone, the higher the number.

For maximum heart rate, the value for each zone is the same as the zone number, whereas for threshold heart rate, the values are different above Zone 4 (see Table 6.7).

A simple formula can be used to arrive at training load:

$$\text{Load} = \text{Intensity} \times \text{Volume (time)}$$

That is, intensity as represented by the weighted value of the heart zone multiplied by the volume of time spent in that heart zone equals training load. The result is your training points.

TABLE 6.8   Training Load and Anchor Heart Rates

Zone	Threshold Heart Rate		Maximum Heart Rate	
	Training Load Value (per min.)	Riding Time, 30 min.	Training Load Value (per min.)	Riding Time, 30 min.
5c*	10	300 points	5	180 points
5b	8	240 points	5	180 points
5a	6	180 points	5	180 points
4	4	120 points	4	120 points
3	3	90 points	3	90 points
2	2	60 points	2	60 points
1	1	30 points	1	30 points

*Zone 5c is 110 to 115 percent of threshold heart rate. Its extreme intensity would not allow someone to stay in this zone for 30 consecutive minutes. It is used here only as an example of the calculation, not as a workout recommendation.

Example: Amanda rides for 30 minutes in Zone 3. Applying the formula $L = I \times V$, she multiplies 3 (the weight for Zone 3) by 30 (minutes) and gets 90 training points for this ride.

In Zones 1 through 4, both maximum and threshold heart rate result in the same number of points for the same workout. Above Zone 4, however, they diverge because of the differences in weight of Zone 5 (maximum) and Zones 5a, 5b, and 5c (threshold). Table 6.8 shows the differences in training load for a thirty-minute ride in each of the zones under the two anchoring methods.

Manipulating Training Load

Having the ability to quantify training load allows you to manipulate the variables—intensity and volume—that go into training load in order to introduce effective periodization into your weekly training plans.

Working with the concept of training load allows you to know exactly how much training is "enough." For example, imagine you put in 10 hours (600

TABLE 6.9   Periodization of Training Load: One Endurance Mesocycle

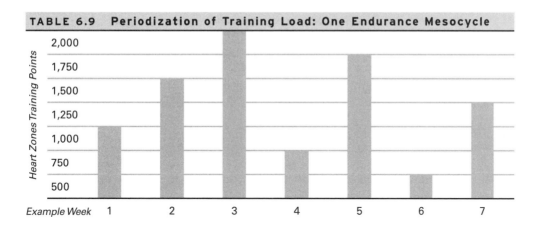

minutes) on the bike last week, and your training plan tells you that you should have accumulated 1,510 training points. You can check your training log and discover that you came close, falling short by only 70 points. How could you have accumulated those additional points? Another 70 minutes in Zone 1, or 35 more minutes in Zone 2, or 20 minutes in Zone 3 plus 5 minutes in Zone 2. . . . In fact, there are endless ways to adjust time and intensity to accumulate a given number of training points. That is the beauty of the Heart Zones Cycling system!

Microcycles: A Mix of High Load and Low Load

The nitty-gritty details of designing each and every microcycle comes in Chapter 8, but we want to give you the theoretical underpinnings of microcycle planning here. The essential point to remember is that, over the course of your macrocycle, the training load varies from one microcycle to the next as well as within each microcycle itself.

At this point, you might be asking yourself, "How do I know when to work hard and when to back off?" Very good question! Here are the basic guidelines about quantity of load (how many training points) to get in each training block:

Preparation 1. Progress from low to moderate load.

Preparation 2. Progress from moderate to high load, then back to moderate.

Event/Competition. Moderate load throughout.

Transition. Low load.

Your next question is likely to be, "How do I know how many points are low, moderate, and high?" The answer depends on the rider. Training load has two variables, intensity and time (volume). As you ride with these two variables in mind, you will soon begin to quantify the combination of time on the bike and intensity level that comprise "low load" for you. For example, a low-load week for you might be 6 hours (360 minutes) on the bike with most of that time in Zone 2. In terms of training points, this would be a load of roughly 720 (2 × 360) points.

On the other hand, a friend of yours might think a low-load week is 6 hours, with most of her time in Zone 3. Putting in a couple of hours in Zone 2, plus 4 hours in Zone 3 gives her a training point total of 960 points. For her, a training load of 960 training points might be a good estimate for a low load for a week.

Can you see why we do not want to prescribe for you a predetermined number of points? What is low load to one rider is moderate load to another rider. You will simply have to get on your bike and experiment until you come up with numbers that work for you.

One more thing: The training load given for a mesocycle or a block is an average of sorts. Within each block, which is made up of microcycles, which are made up of weeks, which are made up of daily rides, you vary the load. In a seven-week mesocycle that calls for "moderate to high" load, some weeks will be high load, some weeks will be moderate load, and some weeks can be low load, as long as the overall load is moderate to high for you.

So, for example, the training load distribution for an event rider who has designed an eight-month macrocycle might look like the one presented in Table 6.10. On the other hand, a competitive rider who has a 48-week macrocycle might distribute training load like the one in Table 6.11.

TABLE 6.10 Training Load for an Event Rider, 36-Week Macrocycle

	Prep 1	Prep 2	Event/Competition	Transition
Purpose	Base and Endurance	Strength and Power	Event Training	Regeneration
Time	8 weeks	8 weeks	16 weeks	4 weeks
Training Load	Mar. Apr.	May June	July Aug. Sept. Oct. 50-miler 100-miler	Nov.

Training Load bars:

Level	Mar.	Apr.	May	June	July	Aug.	Sept.	Oct.	Nov.
High				■					
Medium		■	■			■	■	■	
Low	■				■				■

TABLE 6.11 Training Load for a Competitive Rider, 48-Week Macrocycle

	Prep 1	Prep 2	Event/Competition	Transition
Purpose	Base and Endurance	Strength and Power	Event Training/Racing	Regeneration
Time	12 weeks	8 weeks	20 weeks	8 weeks
Training Load	Jan.–March	March–May	May–Sept.	Oct.–Nov.

Training Load bars:

Level
Highest
Higher
High
Medium High
Medium
Medium Low
Low
Lower
Lowest

To help you periodize and design your training plan, each of the rides found in Appendix A provides you with an estimate of its training points. The exact number will depend on how many minutes you spend in each zone during the ride. As you experience more Heart Zones rides, you will come to love the power and flexibility that result from calculating and manipulating training load.

LET'S RECAP

Here are the basic questions you should answer before moving on to the next chapter:

- What is/are the date(s) of the event(s) for which you are training?
- On what date will you begin your training?
- How many weeks are there between your start date and your event date(s)?
- How many hours do you have available for riding during each week between your start date and your event date(s)? In your notebook or log, try to estimate the number of hours for each week.

After answering those questions, become acquainted with the Training Tree that corresponds to the anchor heart rate you are using (maximum or threshold heart rate). Begin to think about how the Training Tree's "time in zone" guidelines apply to your available training hours and your training goals. Remember, you can make changes to any part of the Heart Zones Cycling program that will make it work better for you and your goals.

Now that you have a better understanding of periodization, you can begin to put all the pieces of the puzzle—your training program—together. That is the topic of the next chapter.

THE THREE-HEARTED CYCLIST

Bobbie Jackson, Heart Zones Cycling Level IV Master Trainer, would like to introduce you to Bill, a unique cyclist: Bill is a fifteen-year heart transplant survivor. He rides daily, eats smart to control his weight, and he cares for his heart—his second heart.

For a long time, Bill had his training ride times and distances down to the exact duration and speed. He would ride for exactly 60 minutes at 10 mph. He never rode faster or farther; at that speed and distance, he was confident that his heart would keep beating just the way it was supposed to. During their early rides together, Bobbie and Bill discussed his surgery, medications, and goals. Bill did not have a training system and he did not use a monitor.

Then one spring day, after a winter of indoor riding on trainers, he decided it was time for a change. He imagined himself riding across his home state of West Virginia. First, he bought a heart rate monitor. Then he met with his cardiologist, who gave him a green light to train for this event. He hired Bobbie as his coach, and he immersed himself into what was for him a new training system that he called his new cycling religion—Heart Zones Cycling. To get started, Bobbie helped Bill find his maximum heart rate and set his five zones.

Because of Bill's medical history and medications, they closely monitored his high-intensity sprints and the quickness of his recovery heart rate numbers. In the beginning of his training, he did not believe that he could go fast and elevate his heart rate without something bad happening, a cardiac incident. However, that was before he knew his zones and how to use them. After about two weeks, Bill phoned Bobbie to say that he had just ridden twenty miles, and at the end of the ride, he rode up two hills to his house without stopping to rest. He had never been able to do that before. Bill told Bobbie, "I'm sure glad you talked to me about Heart Zones Cycling. I'm riding better than I ever thought possible."

Bill has been helped by three hearts: the heart from his generous donor, the heart that Bobbie uses to coach him to be a better cyclist, and the heart of Heart Zones Cycling. As he trains for his big event, the ride across West Virginia, Bill depends on all three of those hearts to accomplish his goal.

PERSONALIZE YOUR TRAINING PROGRAM

In the previous chapters, you learned how to define goals, find your anchor heart rate, set your zones, and periodize your training load. In effect, you have begun to build your training program. This riding program combines the latest technologies with the most recent research about athletic performance and human potential to result in a new and revolutionary approach to your riding.

THE SEVEN-STEP HEART ZONES CYCLING PROGRAM

A training program takes you step-by-step to a short- or long-term goal through the accomplishment of it. Designing and implementing a successful training program is a matter of both art and science. The science of training has grown dramatically in the past few decades; the art of applying the science always lags a bit behind. The art of training requires skills and intuition that come from years of experience with one or more training methodologies.

In the Heart Zones methodology, your training program consists of seven essential steps:

STEP 1. Define your goals.

Determine short- and long-term goals.

Write down the specific desired outcomes.

STEP 2. Find your anchor heart rate.

Determine your maximum heart rate, or

Determine your threshold heart rate.

STEP 3. Set your heart zones according to your anchor heart rate.

STEP 4. Periodize your training load.

- Select the appropriate Training Tree for your anchor heart rate.
- Determine the number of weeks in your macrocycle and each of its mesocycles.
- Calculate your weekly training time budget.
- Distribute time in each heart zone according to the branches of the training tree.
- Calculate and distribute training load according to the rules of periodization.

STEP 5. Design your plan (daily sequence of rides).

STEP 6. Log your progress—record outcomes, thoughts, and analyses of workouts on paper or on your computer.

STEP 7. Assess and adjust.

Test and retest for improvements and training plan modification. Administer assessments every four to twelve weeks and compare results.

One thing needs to be clear at the outset: Training programs and training plans are not the same things. Your Heart Zones Cycling *program* encompasses all aspects of applying the Heart Zone Training methodology in the context of one of the anchoring heart rates. It means that you are applying data you've obtained with the help of technology to manage the totality of your training—the step-by-step progression that leads to your attaining your cycling goals. A training *plan* is just one part of the training program. It tells you what to do and when to do it; the program describes how you do it, how to measure it, and how to adjust it.

THE PROGRAM PRINCIPLES

Your Heart Zones Cycling training program is founded on a set of principles. These principles also apply to the training plan you will put together in the next chapter and are as follows.

Honor your goals. You accomplish best what you can see as an outcome or a process. Keep your goals in mind; take ownership of them; draw motivation from them.

Stay in the zones. Ride in your training zones in accordance with the ride plan. On low-intensity days, ride in Zones 1, 2, and 3, and on high-intensity days, ride in Zones 4 and 5 (5a, 5b, and 5c for threshold riders).

Trust your tools. Your monitor is almost always right. When you see big numbers on the display, yet you "feel" that you are working at low intensity, you are probably wrong and your meter or monitor is probably right.

Follow your plan. Your training plan is your road map. Follow it. If you run into a roadblock or a training problem, modify the plan.

Leverage the power of quantification. Data makes the difference; use the measurements your tools give you to meet your goals.

Keep track of your progress. Your training program must include a way to log your workouts, assessments, competition results, and information about the context of your training—your framework.

Do all seven steps. All the parts of the program work together; each step supports and reinforces all the others. Ignoring any one step weakens the total program and makes it more difficult for you to achieve your cycling goals.

TAKING THE SEVEN STEPS TO SUCCESS

Heart Zone Cycling success depends on your ability to link all the parts of the program together—technology, data, operating principles, and a focus on you and your goals.

How do you put it all together? Let's follow along as one rider, Alberto, follows the seven steps to create a personalized Heart Zones Cycling training program.

Alberto is a "beginning advanced" rider, or a competitive rider. He has raced in two or three events per year for the past five years. He uses his threshold heart rate to anchor his training zones.

Step 1. Define your goals.

Alberto writes down a short-term SMART goal and a long-term SMART goal.

Short-Term Goal: To achieve a personal record (PR) in a 10-mile time trial within the next eighteen weeks (at the end of the Preparation 2 mesocycle). This goal is SMART because it is

   Specific. It specifies what and when.

   Measurable. Beating his current personal record of twenty-six minutes is measurable.

   Action oriented. Strict adherence to the training plan will get him to this new PR.

   Realistic. He can commit to the required twelve hours a week of training.

   Timely. He is ready physically and mentally to work toward and achieve this goal.

Long-Term Goal: To upgrade to a Category 2 rider within the next twelve months. This goal is also SMART because it is

   Specific. It specifies what and when.

   Measurable. He must meet the USCF point requirement to upgrade.

Action oriented. Achieving this goal requires him to follow all aspects of his Heart Zones Cycling training plan and participate in enough races to meet the point requirements.

Realistic. The time commitment is possible.

Timely. Alberto is ready physically and mentally to work toward and achieve this goal.

Step 2. Find your anchor heart rate.

Using the Threshold Cycling Road Test ride (found in Appendix A), Alberto has determined that his cycling threshold heart rate is 145 bpm.

Step 3. Set your heart zones.

From Alberto's threshold heart rate of 145 bpm, he sets his heart zones as follows:

Zone 1:   87–102 bpm
Zone 2:   102–116 bpm
Zone 3:   116–130 bpm
Zone 4:   130–145 bpm
Zone 5a: 145–152 bpm
Zone 5b: 152–160 bpm
Zone 5c: Above 160 bpm

Alberto has a new GPS cycling instrument to keep track of distance, speed, time, altitude, and heart rate. He enters his threshold heart rate as if it were his maximum heart rate, and then he sets it on "percentage" rather than beats per minute. This way, he converts a maximum heart rate monitor into a threshold heart rate monitor. His monitor now shows heart rates above 145 bpm as greater than 100 percent and heart rates below 145 bpm as less than 100 percent.

CAN YOUR HEART RATE MONITOR BE A THRESHOLD MONITOR?

Some monitors do not allow you to go above 100 percent of a number because they are "maximum-only" monitors. You can test your own monitor by programming in a low maximum number to see if the monitor allows you to go above this heart rate point.

If nothing else, you can always resort to programming each of the zones manually. Spend some time with your monitor and see what it will do. You may have an older one-button monitor that does not store time in zone or allow for programming of maximum or threshold heart rate for automatic zone calculation. Tape your threshold heart rate zone column right to your handlebars. As your fitness improves, change the zone column taped to your handlebars and ride in your new threshold zones.

Step 4. Periodize your training load.

Recall that periodizing your training load involves four steps:

STEP 1. Select the appropriate Training Tree for your anchor heart rate (threshold or maximum heart rate).

STEP 2. Determine the number of weeks in your macrocycle and each of its mesocycles.

STEP 3. Calculate your weekly training time budget and time in each zone.

STEP 4. Calculate and distribute training load according to the rules of periodization.

Here is how Alberto begins to think about periodization:

Select the Appropriate Training Tree. Alberto uses the Threshold Training Tree shown in Table 7.1.

Determine the Number of Weeks in the Macrocycle and Its Mesocycles. Alberto has two goals, one short term and one long term. His short-term goal is eighteen weeks away, and his long-term goal is forty weeks away. With a calen-

TABLE 7.1 Heart Zones Training Tree for Threshold

		Zones							
		1	2	3	4		5a	5b	5c
Mesocycle	Branch	Aerobic				Threshold	Nonaerobic		
COMPETITION		10%	20%	30%	35%	—	3%	1%	1%
PREPARATION 2: Event-Specific Training	Power	—	5%	30%	40%	—	15%	7%	3%
	Strength	10%	10%	30%	50%	—	—	—	—
PREPARATION 1: Conditioning and Technique	Endurance	20%	30%	40%	10%	—	—	—	—
	Base	20%	40%	30%	10%	—	—	—	—
TRANSITION		10%	20%	60%	10%	—	—	—	—

dar in hand, Alberto begins to outline his macrocycle using a simple guideline called the 50-50-20 rule: Of the number of weeks between the start of training and the date of the "big goal," 50 percent is for Preparation training, 50 percent is for Competition training, and a number of weeks equal to 20 percent of the start-to-goal training period gets tacked on at the end for Transition.

Alberto applies the 50-50-20 rule: The number of weeks between the start of training and his main goal event is forty weeks, so Alberto designates 50 percent of that time (the first twenty weeks) for Preparation 1 and Preparation 2 training combined, and the subsequent twenty weeks for Competition training. To determine the length of his Transition mesocycle, he calculates 20 percent of forty weeks, which is eight weeks, and tacks that time to the end of the Competition mesocycle. Therefore, his entire macrocycle is forty-eight weeks long.

Would you like to see that 50-50-20 rule one more time? If there are forty weeks between the start of training and the goal event or competition, then

50 percent of 40 weeks = 20 weeks → Preparation 1 and 2 blocks

50 percent of 40 weeks = 20 weeks → Competition block

20 percent of 40 weeks = 8 weeks → Transition block

To further divide the weeks for preparation training into Preparation 1 and Preparation 2, Alberto relies on his own experience to decide that Preparation 1, in which he will build his base and endurance, should be about 60 percent of his preparation training, and Preparation 2, in which he will work on strength and power, should be about 40 percent of his preparation training. Alberto's macrocycle, then, winds up looking like the chart in Table 7.2.

TABLE 7.2 Alberto's Macrocycle

Preparation 1		Preparation 2		Competition (through Goal date of Oct. 15)	Transition
Base	Endurance	Strength	Power	Competition-Specific Skills	Regeneration
6 weeks	6 weeks	3 weeks	5 weeks	20 weeks	8 weeks
1/8–2/18	2/19–3/31	4/1–4/23	4/23–5/27	5/28–10/15	10/16–12/9

Your macrocycle may be longer or shorter than Alberto's 48-week macrocycle. The "advanced beginner" or the event rider might have a training season that lasts five or six months, say, twenty-four or thirty weeks. For a 24-week macrocycle, the 50-50-20 rule would give a macrocycle that looks like the one shown in Table 7.3.

TABLE 7.3 A 24-Week Macrocycle

Preparation 1		Preparation 2		Competition	Transition
Base	Endurance	Strength	Power	Competition-Specific Skills	Regeneration
3 weeks	3 weeks	2 weeks	4 weeks	12 weeks	4–5 weeks
1/8–1/31	2/1–2/21	2/22–3/7	3/8–4/7	4/8–7/1	7/2–8/5

When it comes to designing your macrocycle and its mesocycles, do whatever works best for you, and continually assess and adjust your plan as indicated by your training data.

Calculate a Weekly Training Time Budget and Time in Each Zone. Alberto works forty hours a week (eight hours a day, Monday through Friday). For Preparation 1 and Preparation 2 training he will commit to twelve hours (720 minutes) a week of riding that he will schedule around his job.

Alberto can look at his Training Tree and see how time in each zone should be distributed. For example, for Preparation 1 training, his Training Tree looks like Table 7.4.

TABLE 7.4   Alberto's Training Tree for Preparation 1

Mesocycle	Purpose	Zone 1	Zone 2	Zone 3	Zone 4	Zone 5a,b,c	Weeks
PREPARATION 1	Endurance	20%	30%	40%	10%	—	6 weeks
	Base	20%	40%	30%	10%	—	6 weeks

Knowing his training time budget for each week is 720 minutes, Alberto multiplies 720 times 6 weeks to get 4,320 minutes of total riding time for the Base mesocycle and an equal number of minutes for the Endurance mesocycle. Now he can figure out his time in each zone (time in zone, or TIZ) during this training period (Table 7.5).

TABLE 7.5   Alberto's Training Tree for Preparation 1 with TIZ per Week

Mesocycle	Purpose	Zone 1		Zone 2		Zone 3		Zone 4		Zone 5a, 5b, 5c		Total Minutes	Weeks
		%	min.	%	min.	%	min.	%	min.	%	min.		
PREPARATION 1	Endurance	20%	144	30%	216	40%	288	10%	72	—	—	1,656	6
	Base	20%	144	40%	288	30%	216	10%	72	—	—	1,656	6

Alberto will use the same process to calculate TIZ for each mesocycle during his training season. Some riders are tempted to try to map out TIZ for the entire macrocycle at the beginning of Preparation 1; others, like Alberto, prefer to plan each mesocycle along the way. Alberto has learned that the noncycling aspects of life have a way of changing his plans, so he will wait to figure out TIZ for the other mesocycles later.

Calculate Training Load for Each Mesocycle.   You'll recall that training load is calculated with the formula:

$$Load = Intensity \times Volume\ (time)$$

For the Preparation 1 Base mesocycle, the total training load can be calculated by adding the loads from all the zones in the mesocycle. You will recall that intensity is represented by the "weight" of each zone. You may want to use a table such as Table 7.6 to help with the training load calculations (or create an electronic spreadsheet that will do the calculations for you).

TABLE 7.6   Weekly Training Load for Threshold Preparation 1 Base

Zone	Zone Weight	×	Minutes in Zone	=	Training Points
1	1		144		144
2	2		288		576
3	3		216		648
4	4		72		288
5a	6		—		—
5b	8		—		—
5c	10		—		—
					Total Points = 1,656

Using the training load formula table, Alberto calculates his total training load for the Preparation 1 Base mesocycle for 720 minutes of riding time per week:

(1 × 144 min.) + (2 × 288 min.) + (3 × 216 min.) + (4 × 72 min.) = 1,656 per week

Similarly, Alberto's Preparation 1 Endurance mesocycle has a total training load as follows:

(1 × 144 min.) + (2 × 216 min.) + (3 × 288 min.) + (4 × 72 min.) = 1,728 per week

Distribute Training Load According to the Rules of Periodization. The calculations of training load for the various mesocycles give Alberto a rough idea of what constitutes a "low" week, a "medium" week, and a "high" week for him. The Training Tree is designed to give you a low to moderate load during the Preparation 1 Base mesocycle, so Alberto knows that in a week in which he rides for 720 minutes, accumulating about 1,600 training points is "low" for him. On the other hand, during the Preparation 2 Power mesocycle, the Training Tree will instruct him to ride at much higher intensities. Riding in the higher zones will give him a high number of training points—over 3,000 points per week. With 1,600 points being "low" training load and 3,000 points being "high" training load, Alberto can designate a midrange number of training points as "medium," say, 2,300 training points. Over the course of Preparation 1 and Preparation 2, then, Alberto's training load will increase in the manner shown in Table 7.7.

Knowing what high, medium, and low training loads are for him, Alberto can vary his daily and weekly schedules of rides. He knows that even though the six weeks of Preparation 1 Base training will average about 1,600 training points per week, he should vary his training—some days should have relatively high load, and other days should have relatively low load. Therefore, the six weeks of Preparation 1 Base, which need to average a low to moderate training load, might look like what's depicted in Table 7.8. The weekly training loads bounce around, but they stay well within a low to moderate range, and when averaged over the entire six weeks, the overall training load is "low" for Alberto.

TABLE 7.7   Alberto's Weekly Load Distribution for Preparations 1 and 2

Heart Zones Training Points				
3,000				
2,900				
2,800				
2,700				
2,600				
2,500				
2,400				
2,300				
2,200				
2,100				
2,000				
1,900				
1,800				
1,700				
1,600				
	PREPARATION 1 Base (6 weeks): 1,600 points/week	PREPARATION 1 Endurance (6 weeks): 1,700 points/week	PREPARATION 2 Strength (3 weeks): 2,300 points/week	PREPARATION 2 Power (5 weeks): 3,000 points/week

Looking down the road, Alberto will apply the same steps to the remainder of his macrocycle: Determine TIZ according to the Training Tree, calculate training load per week, and then begin to map out variation over the course of each mesocycle.

What About Maximum Heart Rate as the Anchor?

What if Alberto were using his maximum instead of threshold heart rate to anchor his Heart Zones? What would be different in the steps we've outlined?

TABLE 7.8   Alberto's Preparation 1 Base Periodization Plan

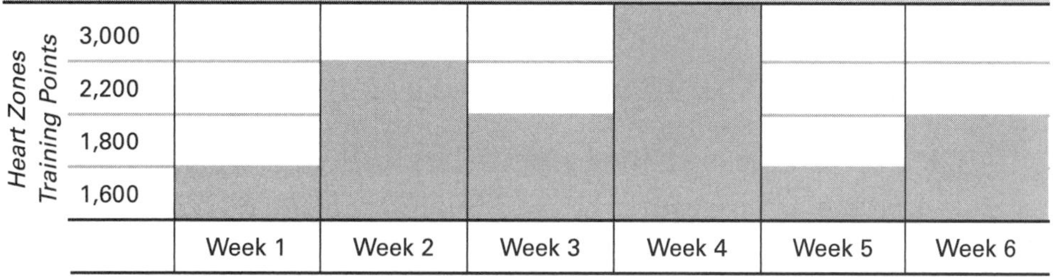

Heart Zones Training Points	Week 1	Week 2	Week 3	Week 4	Week 5	Week 6
3,000						
2,200	1,600	2,200	1,800	3,000	1,600	1,800

Well, everything: His anchor heart rate would be different, his zones would be different, and the calculations of training load would be different. Here is an overview of what Alberto's program would look like if he used his maximum heart rate to anchor his Heart Zones.

Using Maximum Heart Rate as Your Anchor.   First, Alberto would determine his maximum heart rate using one of the assessments provided in Chapter 4 (and in Appendix B). Let's say, for the sake of example, that Alberto's cycling maximum heart rate is 185 bpm.

Setting Heart Zones Based on Maximum Heart Rate.   Knowing that Alberto's maximum heart rate is at 185 bpm, then his Heart Zones would be as follows:

Zone 1: 93–111 bpm
Zone 2: 111–130 bpm
Zone 3: 130–148 bpm
Zone 4: 148–167 bpm
Zone 5: 167–185 bpm

Selecting the Appropriate Training Tree.   Next, Alberto would refer to the Heart Zones Training Tree for maximum heart rate (see Table 6.5, which is also provided in Appendix B).

Determining the Number of Weeks in the Macrocycle and Its Mesocycles.
Alberto's macrocycle and its various mesocycles would look the same regardless of the anchor heart rate he was using.

Calculating Weekly Training Time and TIZ. Alberto's weekly training budget would be the same whether he uses maximum heart rate or threshold heart rate. TIZ is essentially identical as well, although in the threshold system, time in Zone 5 is divided into three subzones: 5a, 5b, and 5c.

Calculating Training Load for Each Mesocycle. Using maximum heart rate differs from threshold when calculating training load for time spent in Zone 5. Compare Table 7.9, which shows the Power branch of the Threshold Training Tree, with Table 7.10, which shows the Power branch of the Maximum Heart Rate Training Tree.

TABLE 7.9 The Power Branch in the Threshold Training Tree

		Zones							
Threshold Heart Rate		1	2	3	4		5a	5b	5c
Mesocycle	Branch		Aerobic			Threshold	Nonaerobic		
PREPARATION 2: Event-Specific Training	Power	—	5%	30%	40%	—	15%	7%	3%

In a week in which Alberto rides 720 minutes, the Maximum Heart Rate Training Tree has him spending 25 percent of that time in Zone 5. That equals 180 minutes. Using the training load formula, training load for that time equals 180 minutes multiplied by a weight of 5, for 900 training points.

On the other hand, in the same week in which Alberto rides 720 minutes, the Threshold Training Tree has him spending 15 percent of his time in Zone 5a (with a zone weight of 6), 7 percent of his time in Zone 5b (with a zone

TABLE 7.10 The Power Branch in the Maximum Heart Rate Training Tree

Maximum Heart Rate		Zones				
		1	2	3	4	5
Mesocycle	Branch		Aerobic		Threshold	Nonaerobic
PREPARATION 2: Event-Specific Training	Power	—	5%	30%	40%	—	25%

weight of 8), and 3 percent of his time in Zone 5c (with a zone weight of 10). TIZ for Zones 5a, 5b, and 5c for the week is the following:

15 percent of 720 minutes = 108 minutes

7 percent of 720 minutes = 50 minutes

3 percent of 720 minutes = 22 minutes

Training load for time spent in Zones 5a, 5b, and 5c is calculated using the training load formula as follows:

(6 × 108 min.) + (8 × 50 min.) + (10 × 22 min.) = 1,268 training points

While the concepts are identical with whichever anchor heart rate and Training Tree you use, the actual calculations for training load will differ somewhat for time spent riding above Zone 4.

AND NOW BACK TO OUR PROGRAM . . .

Armed with an overview of how you will periodize your training load, you are ready to embark on the last three steps of the program:

- Designing your training plan
- Logging your progress
- Assessing and adjusting your plan

Step 5. Design your plan.

Your training plan is your road map. It is the schedule of events—when and where and for how long you get to be on your bike. In fact, it is so important that it gets its own chapter, coming up next.

Step 6. Log your progress.

A ride diary is an invaluable asset to your training program. This tool is a way to permanently record your rides. Logging is powerful because you write it, you maintain it, and you decide what information should be included in it. It takes only a few minutes a day to enter the information into your log, yet the return on your investment is enormous.

A training log is more than just a record-keeping tool. It is useful for analysis and comparisons. It shows you trends and directions. It is a useful way to share information with others, too, and get their feedback, if desired. If you are using a certified coach, your log provides him or her with valuable data and descriptions.

You can record your rides and their accompanying information in a book like the Heart Zones Training Log (see Figure 7.1, which is also located in Appendix B) or on your PC in a client-based log or Web-based application. This service is also provided to you through the Heart Zones Training Center. The key is to use whatever format you feel comfortable with. Try them all to see which one keeps you logging—daily, if possible.

Step 7. Assess and adjust.

The best test of all is performing the event itself—the competition or the ride. That is the proof that the training methodology and the program are working for you. The next-best test of your current fitness and riding level is to periodically and regularly take assessments—field and lab tests—to

Heart Zones Cycling Log

Date	Sport Activity	DST Distance	Time	Time In Zone Z1	Z2	Z3	Z4	Z5	Key Workout Type	Averages	am Heart Rate	Body Weight/Fat	Recovery Heart Rate	Weight Training Time	STRETCH Stretching Time	A, B, C, F Training Rating	∑HZT HZT Points

Summary for the Week — Total Training Time (min): ____ Z1 % | Z2 % | Z3 % | Z4 % | Z5 %

Year-to-Date Summary — Total Training Time (min): ____ Z1 % | Z2 % | Z3 % | Z4 % | Z5 %

AVERAGE OR TOTALS: BPM | LBS. | BPM | MIN. | MIN. | RATING

Notes:

Notes:

FIGURE 7.1 Heart Zones Cycling Log

TABLE 7.11 Assessment Rides by Training Block

	Preparation 1	Preparation 2	Event/Competition	Transition
Hill Sprints	x			
The All-Out Trip	x			
Larger Than Life	x			
Threshold Endurance Road Test	x	x	x	
Threshold Road Cycling Test	x	x	x	
Aerobic Time Trial	x	x	x	
Steady State Ride	x	x	x	
Cycling Economy Test	x	x	x	
Recovery Interval	x	x	x	
Ambient Heart Rate			x	x
Delta Heart Rate			x	x
Recovery Heart Rate			x	x

measure the changes. If the training program is resonating with you, if you are diligently following the seven steps, if you are using your tools of training technology, and if you are dealing with the "whole cyclist" and not just "the ride," then the test results can provide the motivation and the validation of your training investment.

Which tests are the ones that best measure your performance improvements? The answer is "It depends"—it depends on what block of training you are in. When you are in the Transition period, you actually want to get slower because your training load is low and your focus is off-the-bike. When you are in Preparation 1, you want to test for your aerobic base; you want to see if you can you ride longer at lower heart rates but at the same speed. When you are in Preparation 2, focusing on strength and power, you want to measure your time trial speed, your hill-climbing power, and your riding abilities compared with other cyclists in your category. While in the Competition block, you are interested in your recovery heart rate and your ambient heart rate, among other things. In addition, measuring delta heart rate (an orthostatic assessment) is essential to avoiding the potential hazards of overtraining. Delta heart rate is an indicator of your current health and stress conditions. You can find assessments for ambient heart rate, delta heart rate, and recovery heart rate in Appendix C. Table 7.11 lists the assessment rides you will want to use during each of the training blocks.

Assessment leads to adjustment. Exercise scientists have not yet been able to tell us the exact amount of training or the amount of training load that a cyclist should undertake to produce the greatest peak in performance. You will be trying to discover that for yourself as you log, assess, and adjust your training plan in accordance with what your data are telling you. Your challenge as a cyclist is to do the best you can with what you know. Developing your Heart Zones Cycling program alone or with the help of a certified coach or coach mentor is a process. Over time, through trial and error, you will be collecting and analyzing data that helps you discover what kinds of training will produce the best results for you.

THE ESSENTIAL ROLE OF DATA

Information is power, but how do you take advantage of that power in the context of your Heart Zones Cycling program? Data allows you to better manage your long-term planning, short-term planning, and each individual ride. Have a look at two tools, heart rate monitors and power meters, and the role they might play in your planning process.

Your Heart Rate Monitor as Tachometer

In reality, a heart rate monitor is as much a management tool as it is a measuring tool. Your heart rate monitor is the source of an amazing amount of information:

- Are you riding easy enough? On your recovery days, you need to ride in the low zones to allow adequate time for recovery.

- Are you riding hard enough? On your high-intensity days, you need to push into the zones at or above threshold for adaptation to occur.

- Is the planned ride too hard? Some days, you need to back off from the ride schedule and say, "It's just not my day." A good example is a hill workout ride, where you find out that you cannot hit your heart rate percentages regardless of motivation and the perception of the effort. This is the time to listen to your heart and throw in the towel.

- Is the planned ride too easy? You might find that you want to ride harder than the plan prescribes for that day; the monitor serves as a braking mechanism keeping you honest and in the zones.

- Have you recovered between rides? Adequate recovery between rides is essential for the training effect. One way of ensuring this is to take a simple heart rate test during your warm-up. Take your heart rate to 70 percent of your maximum or 80 percent of your threshold for two minutes, and then coast for thirty seconds to see how quickly you recover in that time. A drop of 10–20 bpm is a positive indication that you are rested. If your heart rate does not recover that quickly, drop down a zone in your training, or take the day off from riding hard.

- Have you recovered between intervals? *Intervals* are repeats or repetitions of high intensity followed by recovery time (a drop in intensity). If your recovery time is getting longer with each repeat, it may indicate overtraining or fatigue.

- Are you getting fitter on the bike? Using a heart rate monitor for fitness testing is one of the easiest ways to see real improvement from your training. Do at least one of the fitness assessments described in Chapter 10 as part of your weekly ride time. Log the results and compare them over time.

Of course, the most important thing your heart rate monitor tells you is how fast your heart is beating. It's really more of a tachometer than a speedometer. Like your car's tachometer, your heart rate monitor is assessing the load on your muscular engine; it is not telling you how fast you are going. You can rev up your car engine while it is in neutral and the engine can work hard, but the car remains still. Likewise, you can increase your heart rate with internal and external stress and not make your bike wheel move one revolution—just as in a standing start before the starting gun goes off. (This is called "anticipatory heart rate," in case you were curious.) Your heart rate monitor gives you biofeedback information about how hard your engine is working, not whether it is at or above the speed limit.

Your Power Meter as a Way to Measure Work on the Bike

Many cyclists have a hard time understanding what power meters do exactly. Power meters measure your work on the bike, which is the product of how fast you are going and the amount of force that you exert on the pedal. In other words, power meters measure the force put on the pedal given the speed that you are riding. This translates on the bike into gears and cadence. To generate the most power, you pedal at the highest gear that you can push (force) at the highest cadence.

How about a quick physics lesson? You may even remember this from your high school physics class!

Work is the application of force through a distance:

$$\text{Work} = \text{Force} \times \text{Distance}$$

Power is the amount of work done in a given amount of time:

$$\text{Power} = \text{Work} \div \text{Time}$$

If you put those two ideas together, you see that power is the application of force over a particular distance in a given amount of time:

$$\text{Power} = (\text{Force} \times \text{Distance}) \div \text{Time}$$

We can regroup the factors in the equation, like this:

$$\text{Power} = \text{Force} \times (\text{Distance} \div \text{Time})$$

Interestingly enough, Distance ÷ Time is what we call *velocity* or *speed*. So,

$$\text{Power} = \text{Force} \times \text{Velocity}$$

One last tidbit: Power, the force applied to an object over a given distance in a particular amount of time, is measured in watts. So, yes, you could hook up a lightbulb to your bicycle and make it glow, but that procedure probably belongs in a different book.

To change power, you can change any of the variables that go into power: force, distance, or time. For example, applying force quickly takes more power than applying the same force slowly. See?

Here is an example: You rode a time trial, and at the end of the ride, your average power output was 250 watts per minute. Two weeks later, you repeat the time trial, shaving two minutes off your finishing time. You note that your new power average was 260 watts per minute. You produced more power—which results in riding faster and hence a faster finishing time.

You can increase power output on your bike in three different ways:

- Increase your cadence
- Increase the gear
- Apply more force to the pedals

Power-based training is a concrete way to assess training in a new and meaningful way. The amount of power that you can exert at a specific percentage of your threshold or maximum heart rate (relative power per cardiac cost) is a test of your current level of cycling conditioning. Use this data to assess training improvements over time and to see if your cycle plan is helping you move toward the big payoff day—achieving your race or ride event goal.

Power-based training provides an accurate assessment of how effective your body is performing. Comparing one ride with another using power output data is essential to better evaluate your training plan. Exercise physiologist Ed Burke writes in *Serious Cycling:*

> Through the use of a heart rate–power system, you will see significant improvement in race performance when you begin training with power. Applying each of these intensity monitoring systems has the potential to dramatically improve training and racing.

If you are doing the same workouts at the same heart rate but with a higher output, your cycle fitness is improving. If you are doing the same workouts at a lower heart rate but your power output is staying the same, your fitness is improving.

Conversely, if you are doing the same workouts at the same heart rate but at a lower power output, your cycle fitness is declining. And if you are doing the same workout at a lower heart rate but your power output is declining, you are losing fitness.

Strength training coupled with hill workouts and cadence drills can help to improve your power output. If you want to pay attention to power during the ride, be aware that changes in power output during a ride are substantial. Wattage fluctuates rapidly and frequently during the ride, so some riders prefer to look at the data *after* the ride and use the more stable heart rate number during the actual workout itself.

ABIDE BY THE COMMANDMENTS

Before you leave this chapter, let us impart these words of wisdom: Keep the big picture in mind at all times. Hold the vision of your goal before you as you ride, stay excited about this new way of riding, get good use out of your tools, use data to its full advantage, and look forward to logging and reevaluating your progress. To help you remember all this, get out your metaphorical stone tablets and start chiseling, for we close with The Heart Zones Cycling program commandments in Table 7.12.

TABLE 7.12 The Heart Zones Cycling Program Commandments

	"Thou shalt . . ."	*Cycling Example*
I.	Set goals that start from the heart.	What's really important to me is that I maintain balance in my life as I train for my big race.
II.	Select positive goals that, like a magnet, pull you toward them.	Next Sunday, I will pull the pack for at least three minutes rather than drafting the entire ride.
III.	Train on the bike the new way using the new formula of metabolic fitness plus emotional fitness plus physical fitness.	Because I have high cholesterol, I will have it checked every six months as I adjust my diet to fit my new training goals.
IV.	Get out of your comfort zone and try new training systems.	I know that if I do the same thing over and over, I will have the same outcome. So I will buy a more advanced heart rate monitor that also has GPS data for me to use for feedback. I need more feedback because I know that it will help me do better on the bike.
V.	Be realistic about what is achievable as a cycling goal.	Last year, I set my three-mile testing time trial at 20 mph and didn't achieve that. My goal is to train differently this year using the new way so I can hit that number—20 mph—by June 1.
VI.	Train your training program and not that of another.	I control my training rides, not the group. If Tom wants to fly off the front in a sprint, I do not have to chase him down on the Sunday rides. I agree with myself, my ego, and my friends to ride my ride and not theirs.
VII.	Be specific about the racing and training goals.	As I go through my annual goal-setting process, I will be detailed about who, what, when, where, how, and why I am setting each goal. My goal is to set better goals.
VIII.	Use cycling power tools to manage the training program.	I do not have a downloadable distance/speed/heart rate monitor. I will buy one in the next 60 days. I know that if I can compare my time trial rides and computer-generated profiles of each ride, I can use it as a feedback tool and get better results.

(continues)

TABLE 7.12   The Heart Zones Cycling Program Commandments *(continued)*

"Thou shalt . . ."	*Cycling Example*
IX. Measure in order to manage the training plan.	I will keep a ride log and save every workout from my downloadable heart rate monitor so that I have the data to manage my ride progress. I will review my results, and if I cannot interpret them, I will seek professional help.
X. Keep up on the latest information on cycling in order to be a more educated rider.	I shall subscribe to cycling magazines, watch cycling videos, attend cycling expos and events, join my local cycling club, and help others to learn more about cycling because doing so will make me a better rider.
XI. Reevaluate all goals periodically, and reset them to fit the circumstances.	I shall place in the top five at the state road race in my age group in August and will perform time trials and race tests to monitor my progress toward achieving a peak performance on that day. To accomplish this goal, I know that every first Monday of the month, I need to review my goals.

DESIGN YOUR
TRAINING PLAN

Salespeople in the cycling business will tell you that fitting people for a new bike for performance and comfort is a challenge because no two bodies are the same. Similarly, there is no single perfect training plan for everyone. Like bikes, all ride plans should be customized to fit the individual.

We all need a training plan that fits our unique physiology, interests, cycling experience, fitness level, work requirements, time availability, and so forth. You cannot design the same ride plan for everyone because each person has unique performance capacities. Yet it is amazing how often cycling groups try this "one size fits all" approach. Coaches and trainers put packs of riders or groups of individuals together, make them follow the same ride plan, and expect them all to do well. The coach, trainer, or instructor writes the ride prescription such that everyone on the team or in the group does the same intensity, duration, and frequency—the same load and the same rides. Some do well, and others do not. If there are a few stars on the team or in the group who lose a lot of weight or win a race, the coach is considered brilliant. But if some participants don't accomplish their goals, we don't say that the coach is a failure. We should. The coach has failed the group if he or she has not individualized the program and the plan to meet each person's unique needs.

In contrast, the Heart Zones seven-step program is based on your individual physiology—your Heart Zones, anchored by your maximum heart rate or threshold heart rate. Heart Zones Training honors your individual goals, individual physiology, unique sports history, functional capacity, interests, and personal needs; in other words, your framework—you, the rider. In the Heart Zones Training methodology, time on the bike and off the bike is completely about *you*. Your heart sets the tempo, the rhythm, and the pace.

YOUR ROAD MAP

Sally Edwards has a favorite saying: "Plan the work, work the plan, and the plan works!" So what is a training plan, exactly? A training plan is a road map and a schedule. You already know what a road map is—a visual representation of places, distances, directions, size of towns, and the type of roads you will travel. A road map gives you an idea of where you are and where you have to go. Similarly, a training plan is a visual representation of where you are starting from, the places that you are going to travel through, the types of rides that are going to get you from the start to the finish, the distance or time that it is going to take, the days that you are going to ride (the schedule), and the directions to get there. The road map to riding your best is a training plan designed for, about, and centered on you.

Riders are accustomed to using road maps. If we head out for a bike ride into new territory, we not only look at a map in advance to prepare for the ride but take it with us. If we get lost or take the wrong route on the ride, we consult our road map. If we run into a roadblock, we consult our road map. And if we have to change course for whatever reason, we consult our road map. A training plan is no different. It keeps us on the route.

Actually, a training plan is more than a map; it is a map and a schedule. Your training schedule sets up your riding from the macro down to the micro,

EVERY HEART ZONES RIDE . . .

- has a purpose, a physiological goal.

- has a training load, the stress level of the ride.

- is in specified heart zones.

- is based on the rider's current fitness level.

- fits into a ride plan.

- is logged or recorded.

- helps distribute load as prescribed by your Training Tree.

- has a specific duration.

- is one of four types of rides: interval, steady state, combination, or recovery.

- utilizes one or more energy systems.

from the starting line to the finish line and back to the starting line. The training plan schedules all of your rides to add or decrease training load—the riding stress—so that the body adapts to the training stimulus the way you want it to: to get faster, ride farther, and get fitter. In large part, training is about the sequencing of proper stress, optimum recovery, and proper stress again that leads to adaptations, all resulting in the "training effect" of getting fitter. In fact, that is what periodization is all about.

You need a training plan, so where are you going to get it? What does it look like? What is involved here?

There are three different ways to obtain your training plan, and each one has advantages. First, you can design your own; this is called the *self-coaching model*. This book gives you all of the tools you need to successfully design your own ride plan. Becoming a self-coached rider is one of the highest compliments that you can give yourself. It means that you are taking on the challenge of learning to train so you can train forever.

Second, you can hire a coach or a trainer who can write a training plan for you. This choice is popular because it puts some, if not most, of the responsibility on the coach to get to know you *and* to know the Heart Zones Training program you are using. Heart Zones USA has certified coaches who are experts at using these ride plans. They are available to work with you by phone, e-mail, fax, Web, or possibly in person or in a group; you can get in touch with one at www.HeartZones.com.

Finally, you can use "canned" programs that are printed monthly in cycling publications, posted on Web sites, and made available to purchase, usually from a cycling training company. Canned programs are not individualized to you. You are left on your own to follow them or adapt them the best that you can. Clearly, the first two options lead to your highest opportunity for success.

In the Heart Zones Training methodology, your plan is based on the Heart Zones Principles discussed in Chapter 1. Everything about the rides—how they are organized, the quantification and progression of training load, and their flexibility—is centered on you, the rider. That is why they do what you want them to do—help you achieve your goals on the bike.

PUTTING YOUR RIDE PLAN TOGETHER

In the Heart Zones Cycling program, the ride schedule is a daily, weekly, monthly, and yearly posting of your rides and other supporting activities and materials. Your ride schedule shows you a daily overview of your rides over a period of time, usually for four to eight weeks in advance.

A ride plan is like a puzzle, with several pieces that all have to fit together properly in order for you to reach your cycling goal. The information you need to put the pieces together comes from several different sources, including a few you have already become familiar with, such as your Training Tree, your macrocycle and its various mesocycles, your sense of your personal fitness level, and your physiological data such as your maximum heart rate or threshold heart rate. Constructing your ride plan involves selecting individual rides that meet your training needs at the right time and in the proper sequence.

Rules to Train By

Ride longer distances at lower intensities to develop a big base; the bigger the base, the higher the peak. This rule is the basis of the Training Tree. Interestingly, the optimum volume of base training to produce the highest peak has never been quantified by researchers, but the personal experiences of thousands of athletes prove the rule is sound.

More is not *better.* Train with specificity for the minimum amount of time at the appropriate intensities that allow you to achieve your maximum physiological goals. Exceeding the minimum volume of training necessary does not necessarily improve performance and can lead to overtraining.

Daily variability in riding avoids monotony and keeps you fresh. Day-to-day riding variations in training load, courses, and other variables result in more effective adaptation to training. Remember, very long rides even at low intensity are just as demanding as short, high-intensity rides. Hard days can come from either volume or intensity.

Train hard on the hard days and easy on the easy days. Use a heart rate monitor or power meter to quantify your intensity. Easy days mean short rides at low intensity or wattage. When in doubt, always do less on the easy days; training too much on the easy days is more likely to cause negative results than overdoing it on the hard days. Listen to your body! Use your tools! When you are fatigued, do not train hard—no matter what your plan says.

Ride in the right zones at the right time to get the right results. Riding intensity is probably the single most important factor in optimum training. The right intensity is individual to your ability and level of load tolerance. Most people respond quickly to high-intensity training. Remember that racing is usually in Zone 4 and Zone 5, so when you are racing a lot, you may need little or no high-intensity training.

Select Rides for Your Training Block

You have been digesting a lot of information in this book, and it may seem a bit overwhelming. But have no fear—this is where it all starts to make sense. The first step in constructing your ride plan is to have in front of you two things: your Training Tree and Table 8.1, Rides by Training Block. (This table is also located in Appendix B.) Identify the training block or mesocycle in

TABLE 8.1   Rides by Training Block

Block 1 PREP 1 Conditioning/Technique	Block 2 PREP 2 Event Specificity	Block 3 COMPETITION Event Training/Racing	Block 4 TRANSITION Regeneration
Cadence Drills	Cadence Drills	Cadence Drills	Easy Rider 1
Crisscross Zone 2	Comin' Round the Mountain	Comin' Round the Mountain	Crisscross Zone 2
Crisscross Zone 3	Pyramid Scheme 2	Pyramid Scheme 2	Pyramid Scheme 1
Rock Steady	Turtle Rock	Turtle Rock	Steady State Ride
Easy Rider 1	Cruisin'	Cruisin'	Easy Rider 2
Easy Rider 2	Easy Rider 2	Easy Rider 2	
Easy Rider 3	Easy Rider 3	Easy Rider 3	
Turtle Rock	Galactic	Galactic	
Pyramid Scheme 1	Head for the Hills	Head for the Hills	
Steady State Ride	Holy Smokes	Holy Smokes	
Fix It	Kowabunga	Kowabunga	
Recovery Interval	Rock Steady	Hiccup	
Comin' Round the Mountain	Copy Cat	Copy Cat	
	Sign Here, Press Hard	Sign Here, Press Hard	
	Silver Streak	Silver Streak	
	Crisscross Zone 4	Crisscross Zone 4	
	Hiccup		
	Fix It		
	Recovery Interval		

which you are training and the branch of the Training Tree on which you are working, and then learn about the rides that correspond to that branch.

Once you have identified the rides that fit within your block and branch, you can select the appropriate ride for each day based on its type, purpose, and intensity levels.

Select the Right Type of Ride

Every ride fits into a genre or "type." Just like your MP3 player has genres for music such as rock, easy listening, and rhythm and blues, your training program calls for certain genres of rides at certain times. These genres or types of rides are based on what you *do on the bike*. The Heart Zones methodology uses four types of rides:

- Steady State
- Interval
- Recovery
- Combination

Classifying rides based on what you *do* on the bike may be new to you if you are an experienced cyclist. In the past, rides have been categorized based on their primary adaptation. A *primary adaptation* is the physiological benefit or outcome from completing a certain ride type. In the old way of riding, ride types were based on the primary adaptation rather than what you actually do on the bike. In the old way, an "endurance ride" would mean that you were trying to create an endurance adaptation as the physiological benefit. In the new way of riding, the physiological benefit is important because it is an outcome, but it is *not* a ride *type*. In the new way of riding, types of rides are based on intensity: riding continuously steady state, riding with alternating intensities (intervals), riding with low intensity (recovery), and riding with a mixture of the different types (combinations) of intensities. The four Heart Zones ride types are described in Table 8.2.

TABLE 8.2 The Four Basic Ride Types

Ride Type	Description
STEADY STATE	A ride in which the heart rate or training rate is maintained at a constant intensity, speed, or rate of work. Typically, these rides are done at a submaximum intensity level to develop the aerobic system.
INTERVAL	A ride that consists of durations of given intensities followed by durations of rest or recovery. Interval rides vary in intensities to develop both aerobic and nonaerobic systems.
COMBINATION	A ride that includes both steady state and interval training. These rides may include specific training and skill development such as sprinting or climbing, or they may be less structured, such as in a group ride where you are riding in multiple zones at varying speeds.
RECOVERY	A ride that is done at low intensity in the small chainring on a flat course. The intent is to allow your cycling muscles, nervous system, and cardiovascular system to perform an active recovery. The harder you train, the more recovery you will need both on and off the bike.

Selecting the right type of ride means choosing a ride that works on the right set of skills and gives you the right kind of intensity as called for by your Training Tree.

Select Rides Related to Your Physiological Goal

Accomplishing goals is a huge part of the Heart Zones Training methodology. It is a core principle that supports every aspect of your training program. The very meaning of the word *training* includes the idea of riding to reach one or more physiological goals. Physiological goals are outcome goals—they are measurable. For example, during your Preparation 1 training, you ride to improve your endurance and aerobic capacity. Your progress toward your goal is measurable. If your endurance improves by 10 percent and that is what your goal called for, congratulations—you just achieved that physiological goal!

As you begin to read the details of the rides, you will notice that they encompass one or more of the following components of training:

- Short speed work to improve leg speed and form
- Longer intervals at a race pace to improve VO_2max
- Intervals of twenty to forty minutes or longer at threshold to improve lactate threshold and lactate tolerance
- Long rides to build endurance
- Periods of recovery to allow for adequate muscular repair and maximum effort on hard training days

What is really going on during these various components of training? At a high level, all the rides help a cyclist to develop the cardiovascular system both aerobically and nonaerobically so that he or she can ride farther and faster. To do that, the cyclist must also develop his or her muscular strength, muscular endurance, speed (both bike speed and leg speed), and power. The extent to which these physiological processes develop depends on the rider, the goal, and the plan. According to Jack Daniels, a noted exercise physiologist, the following physiological processes need to be optimally developed in order to maximize competitive performance:

- The body's ability to transport blood and oxygen must be improved.
- The ability of the muscles to use the available oxygen effectively must be increased.
- Aerobic capacity, VO_2max, must be increased.
- Power must be improved to get faster.
- The energy demand of the sport must be lowered (in other words, cycling economy improved).

These benefits or adaptations are the result of understanding you, the rider, and manipulating three training principles: frequency, intensity, and time. This manipulation is the part of the planning process in which you select and refine riding protocols that help you to achieve the appropriate physiological goals at the proper time and in the proper sequence. Your Training

Tree gives you guidelines for what kinds of physiological goals to work on and when to work on them. It is up to you to select the rides that work with your schedule and your needs and your physiology, and to execute the rides in a way that will give you the amount of training load you want.

Physiological Energy Systems

Different types of intensity relate to three different physiological energy systems:

- Aerobic energy
- Nonaerobic energy
- ATP-CP energy

Energy system relates to fuel. The fuel that you are using depends on how hard you are riding—in other words, in which zone you are riding. Aerobic energy is used in the cooler, lower zones when there is sufficient oxygen to breathe comfortably and carry on a conversation. In an aerobic ride, the primary source of energy is fat, with less contribution from carbohydrates. On the other hand, nonaerobic energy (also known as *nonoxidative* or *anaerobic energy*) is used when there is insufficient oxygen to breathe comfortably, breathing is labored, and carrying on a conversation is difficult. In a nonaerobic ride, you burn some fat, but the majority of your fuel is coming from carbohydrates. Finally, ATP-CP energy is used for short, explosive power that is ten seconds or less in duration. All three energy systems are important for you, the cyclist, and are used for different types of rides at different types of intensities.

Between two of the intensities, aerobic and nonaerobic, is a neat little space. This space is narrow, dynamic, and very important! It is an *energy system threshold*, the doorway between aerobic and nonaerobic energy systems. The term *threshold* has a lot of different definitions, and we can measure threshold in a lot of different ways. Depending on how we measure it, sometimes it is called the *ventilatory threshold*; other times, the *lactate threshold*. However you want to measure it, threshold is the crossover point when your body switches from using aerobic energy to using nonaerobic energy. It is an important heart rate point or energy space for anyone seeking to become a fitter rider. Training at threshold expands VO_2 capacities, increases the rate of oxygen delivery to the muscles, and progressively improves what is known as *lactate shuttle* (the ability of lactate to move in and out of muscle cells easily in order to provide an energy source to those cells).

Raising your threshold heart rate point closer to your maximum heart rate is an indication that your training program is working—that your physiology is responding positively to training stress. In other words, you are getting fitter. For example, early on in your riding, your threshold heart rate number might be 150 bpm. Ten weeks later, after following a training program, your threshold heart rate number might increase to 160 bpm. This is the positive training effect in action.

How do you relate what your Training Tree suggests you need to the types of rides you will want to select? Begin by thinking about the physiological improvements associated with each of the three energy systems—aerobic, nonaerobic, and ATP-CP. (Remember to refer to the Glossary for clarification about any terms that might be new to you.)

Riding Using the Aerobic Energy System.   Riding in the lower zones stresses the aerobic system in order to build aerobic capacity.

Physiological Goals:
- Stimulate the Type 1 (slow-twitch) muscle fibers to work with less fatigue
- Improve aerobic power of the primary muscles used in cycling, so there is less need to use accessory muscles
- Increase the ability of the muscles to use oxygen through increased mitochondria density
- Improve the heart's efficiency through increased cardiac output
- Increase capillary density in the muscles

- Improve neuromuscular efficiency in terms of pedaling mechanics
- Increase the body's ability to store carbohydrates
- Improve the body's use of fat as a fuel at lower intensities
- Enhance the body's ability to spare endogenous carbohydrate stores because of increased fat utilization
- Increase oxidative enzymes
- Improve muscular endurance
- Lower heart rate at a given workload
- Result in faster speed or higher power output at a given heart rate
- Increase the size and strength of the heart
- Shift the threshold at which work becomes non-oxidative, which results in less need for nonoxidative function and less lactic acid buildup
- Decrease the resting heart rate
- Improve aerobic capacity—raises VO_2max and enhances oxygen transport
- Increase the ability of the cycling muscles to use the available oxygen effectively
- Improve the body's ability to transport blood and oxygen
- Raise threshold for improved lactate tolerance
- Improve cycling speed
- Improve your cycling economy (see the Cycling Economy Test in Appendix A)

Riding Using the Nonaerobic Energy System.   Riding in the higher zones stresses the nonaerobic system which builds nonoxidative capacity.

Physiological Goals:
- Improve VO_2max and the ability to maintain a high steady state speed or power output
- Enhance lactate tolerance and muscle buffering capacity
- Improve fatigue resistance at race pace
- Improve pain tolerance to high-intensity stress

■ Improve neuromuscular recruitment patterns at race pace
■ Increase speed or power output at threshold intensity
■ Raises the threshold heart rate number
■ Enlarge the fat-burning range by raising threshold

Riding Using the ATP-PC Energy System. Training your body to perform at maximum intensity for short periods of time.

Physiological Goals:
■ Increase ATP-PC output to improve high-resistance movements
■ Increase ATP-PC output to improve high-speed bursts
■ Improve rhythm and coordination during maximal efforts
■ Increase muscular strength and nonaerobic power output
■ Improve power starts and finishes
■ Increase glycolytic enzyme activity

When does each energy system kick in? Check out Table 8.3.

TABLE 8.3 Energy Sources for Different Duration Rides

	Ride Duration					
ENERGY SYSTEM	35 seconds to 2 minutes	2–10 minutes	10–30 minutes	30–90 minutes	90 minutes to 3 hours	> 3 hours
Aerobic energy	47%–60%	70%–80%	75%–80%	85%–90%	97%–99%	99%
Nonaerobic energy	53%–40%	20%–30%	20%–25%	10%–15%	1%–3%	0
ATP-CP energy	10%–50%	0	0	0	0	0

To select a particular ride based on energy system and length of interval, you can use a tool called the Ride-O-Gram, shown in Table 8.4. To see which energy systems a ride utilizes, as well as the other selection criteria, you can refer to the Heart Zones Ride Selection Criteria Chart in Table 8.5. (Tables 8.4 and 8.5 can also be found in Appendix B.)

TABLE 8.4 Heart Zones Ride-O-Gram

	Aerobic			Threshold	Nonaerobic					ATP-PC		
	Steady State Intervals (longer period of sustained heart rate)				Medium to Long Intervals (>60 sec.)					Short Intervals (<60 sec.)		
	Muscular Strength	Tempo	Endurance Recovery/Neuro-muscular	Threshold	Hill Sprints	Climbing Acceleration	Non-aerobic Power	VO_2	Race Simulation	Power Starts	PC Jumps	Sprints
Muscular Strength		Turtle Rock	Cadence Drills	Kowabunga	Hill Sprints	Head for the Hills	Holy Smokes	Holy Smokes	Copy Cat	Blowout	Blowout	Silver Streak
Kowabunga		Comin' Round the Mountain	Criss-cross Zone 3	Pyramid Scheme 2	Hiccup	Silver Streak	Pyramid Scheme 2	Pyramid Scheme 2			Jumpin' Jiminie	Pyramid Scheme 2
Comin' Round the Mountain		Criss-cross Zone 3	Criss-cross Zone 4	Cruisin'	Copy Cat		Silver Streak	Copy Cat				Copy Cat
Silver Streak		Rock Steady	Rock Steady	Galactic			Blowout	Blowout				
Blowout		Blowout	Easy Rider 1	Silver Streak								Sign Here, Press Hard
Criss-cross Zone 4		Jumpin' Jiminie	Easy Rider 2	Blowout								
Fix It			Easy Rider 3	Criss-cross Zone 4								Easy Rider 3
			Pyramid Scheme 1									
			Fix It									

TABLE 8.5 Heart Zones Ride Selection Criteria

	Type of Ride: Interval (I), Steady State (SS), Combination (C), Recovery (R), Threshold HR Test (TT), Maximum HR Test (MT), or Assessment (A)	Intensity: Aerobic (A), Threshold (T), Nonaerobic (NA), or ATP-PC (ATP)	Mesocycle: Prep 1 (P1), Prep 2 (P2), Competition (C), or Transition (T)	Duration (minutes)	Terrain: Flat (F), Rolling (R), Hills (H), or Varied (V)
RIDES					
Blowout	C	A, T, NA, ATP	P2, C	90–150	F, R
Cadence Drills and Skills	I	A	P1, P2	60–90	F
Comin' Round the Mountain	C	A	P1, P2, C	90–180	F, R, H
Crisscross Zone 2	I	A	P1	60–150	F, R
Crisscross Zone 3	I	A	P1	60–180	F, R
Crisscross Zone 4	I	T, NA	P2, C	60–180	R
Cruisin'	I	T	P2, C	50–90	F
Copy Cat	C	A, T, NA, ATP	P2, C	90–240	V
Easy Rider 1	R	A	P1, T	30–120	F, R
Easy Rider 2	C, R	A	P1, P2, T	30–120	F, R
Easy Rider 3	C, R	A	P1, P2	50–120	F, R
Fix It	C	A	P2, C	60–120	F, R
Galactic	SS	T	P2, C	60–120	F, R
Head for the Hills	I	NA	P2, C	60–90	H
Hiccup	I	NA	P2, C	90–150	H
Holy Smokes	I	A	P2, C	60–90	F, R
Jumpin' Jiminie	C	A, ATP	P2, C	90–150	F, R
Kowabunga	C	A	P2, C	90–150	F, R, H
Pyramid Scheme 1	I	A	P1	60–100	F, R
Pyramid Scheme 2	I	A, T, NA	P2, C	70–100	F, R
Rock Steady	SS	A	P1, P2	60–150	F, R
Sign Here, Press Hard	I	A, NA, ATP	P2, C	60–180	F, R
Silver Streak	C	A, T, NA, ATP	P2, C	60–180	V
Turtle Rock	SS	A	P1, P2, C	75–180	F, R

(continues)

Zones Ride Selection Criteria *(continued)*				
ᴐ of Ride: Interval (I), Steady State (SS), Combination (C), Recovery (R), Threshold HR Test (TT), Maximum HR Test (MT), or Assessment (A)	Intensity: Aerobic (A), Threshold (T), Nonaerobic (NA), or ATP-PC (ATP)	Mesocycle: Prep 1 (P1), Prep 2 (P2), Competition (C), or Transition (T)	Duration (minutes)	Terrain: Flat (F), Rolling (R), Hills (H), or Varied (V)
ASSESSMENTS				
Aerobic Time Trial	A	A	P1, P2, C	45–60	F, R
Cycling Economy Test	A	A	P1, P2, C	60	H
Hill Sprints	MT	NA	P1	45	H
Larger Than Life	MT	NA	P1	45	F
Recovery Interval Ride	A	A, T, NA	P1, P2, C	50–110	F, R
Steady State Ride	A	A	P1, P2, C	30–90	F, R
The All-Out Trip	MT	NA	P1	60	F
Threshold Cycling Road Test	TT	T	P1, P2, C	75–90	F
Threshold Endurance Road Test	A	T	P1, P2, C	45–100	F

Trainability and Training Tolerance

Distributing appropriate amounts of training load is highly individual. When you first begin to periodize your training load, it is going to take a considerable amount of adjusting your training load up or down over the course of your training plan as you become increasingly aware of two factors: your trainability and your training tolerance.

Trainability is reflected in how quickly your body responds or adapts to the training load. The more trainable your body is, the more quickly you will see physiological changes, such as a positive shift of your threshold heart rate, improved VO_2max, and positive metabolic changes in response to your work on the bike. No two riders have exactly the same degree of trainability. When two different cyclists ride the same number of hours, the same distances, on identical bikes, on the same course, one will get fitter faster than the other. One is more "trainable," physiologically speaking.

Training tolerance is your body's ability to cope with increasing dosages of riding workload. When two different cyclists undertake the same training plans with identical workouts, very often one will get injured, catch colds, and feel fatigued, while the other will progress beautifully toward his or her training goals. Different training tolerances demand different training plans.

WHAT IS THE OPTIMUM TRAINING LOAD?

What is the ideal number of Heart Zones training points? How many points are too many? What is the lowest number you can get and still stay fit?

There is no standard answer to these questions because it depends on many factors, such as your trainability and your past experience. Each person has an individual workload threshold or a quantifiable amount of riding stress that he or she can sustain. Heart Zones training points in a week may range from 300 points to more than 6,000 points. Higher points do not mean that you are a better athlete or faster or fitter, but that your tolerance of exercise quantity is higher. Training load thresholds vary greatly among individuals. For example, Sally Edwards averaged 3,000 Heart Zones Training points a week for the final four weeks prior to her team competition in the Race Across America (RAAM). This was the training load that optimized her physiology.

Riders logging their training points over time are better able to predict when they will reach their peak performance level or when they are training to the point of injury or overtraining. By calculating and tracking training load accurately, you can train at different weekly point levels to determine just how much, how hard, and how long you as an individual can ride to optimize your physiology.

As you progress through your periodized training plan, you must monitor your own trainability and training tolerance, modifying the plan as you go to reach maximize performance while minimizing risk of injury and illness.

The Role of Recovery Heart Rate

Part of the planning process is selecting rides that ensure you are performing a sequence of physiological stresses and periods of recovery. This stress-recovery sequence results in improvement of your riding energy systems. For training to lead to improved fitness, you must apply an appropriate cycle of physical stress and recovery to obtain the training effect.

There are two types of recovery heart rate. *Intrarecovery* heart rate occurs between sets of interval sessions during a single ride. *Interrecovery* heart rate is measured between workout days and daily recovery episodes.

Recovery is the ability of your physiological system to return to a normal (preexercise) state. Depending on the type of physical stress applied and the dosage, recovery can be immediate or take as long as several days or weeks to occur.

Both interrecovery and intrarecovery times can be used to measure your fitness improvements because the longer the elapsed time for either type of recovery, the greater the need for your body to rest or regenerate. You can assess your intrarecovery heart rate using the Interval Recovery Ride assessment located in Chapter 10.

Here are a few simple rules to follow when using recovery times and recovery heart rate to improve your training:

RULE 1. The harder the workout, the longer the recovery time needed. This rule applies to high-intensity, hot, hard training rides. If you spend long periods of time at threshold intensity and above—in other words, in Zone 5—you must allow for a longer recovery. High Heart Zones are physiologically stressful, but it is appropriate to train there as long as you complement them with recovery rides in the lower Heart Zones. A good way to assess whether you have achieved sufficient interrecovery is to measure your resting heart rate when you first wake up in the morning, before getting out of bed. If your resting heart rate is within 5 bpm of normal, you have probably recovered adequately. If not, modify your workouts for the day.

RULE 2. Inability to recover indicates insufficient recovery time.

If your heart rate does not recover between workouts, you may be approaching or in a state of overtraining, or you may not have recovered from the previous ride. You could be experiencing some effects of medication or environmental conditions, or your immune system might be compromised. Or you may be feeling physiological effects from other life stresses such as family pressure or time challenges.

RULE 3. Shortened intrarecovery time means better conditioning.

Between intervals, measure the time required for your heart rate to recover to a designated percentage of maximum heart rate or threshold heart rate. If this period decreases from week to week, you are probably improving your cardiovascular conditioning; it shows your body can recover more quickly from a period of physical stress. This is exactly the kind of physiological improvement you want and makes for a great goal as you train for higher levels of fitness.

A CLOSER LOOK AT HEART ZONES RIDES

Each of the rides described later in this book share similar characteristics: They each have four parts, they are designed to be tailored to the fitness level of the rider, and they are specific to the anchor heart rate (maximum or threshold) the rider is using.

The Three Parts of a Ride

Heart Zones rides all have three parts: warm-up, main set, and cool-down. The rides are classified according to the main set, which is the primary ride period. The distribution of your ride time into these three different parts usually looks something like this:

Warm-up: About 15 percent of ride time

Main set: About 70 percent of ride time

Cool-down: About 15 percent of ride time

The Fitness Level of the Rider

As you become more familiar with the Heart Zones rides, you will see that they are designed to fit each rider according to his or her fitness level. Fitness level is subjective. Reading the descriptions of each fitness level in Table 8.6, identify the one that best describes your current fitness level.

The Training Load of the Ride

Each Heart Zones ride is designed to offer you a wide range of training points, depending on how long you want to ride and/or how many times you want to repeat intervals. As you move up and across your Training Tree, as your fitness improves, you can increase the duration of each part of the ride and add more repetitions to increase the training load.

HOW TO "READ" A HEART ZONES RIDE

As you can see by looking at the rides, the write-ups for almost all Heart Zones rides have the same four sections:

- Ride selection criteria
- Set by rider's fitness level
- Heart rate profile and rider's notes
- Ride overview

The Ride Selection Criteria give you the information you need when selecting a ride for a particular day: what type of ride it is (steady state, interval,

TABLE 8.6   Five Fitness Levels of Riders

Level 1	Distance	Can ride 5–20 miles at moderate intensity
	Time	Can ride 20–60 minutes without stopping
	Speed	Comfortable speed is under 14 mph
	Experience	Rode less than 3 hours per week in the past year
Level 2	Distance	Can ride 20–50 miles at moderate intensity
	Time	Can ride more than 60 minutes without stopping
	Speed	Comfortable speed is about 14–16 mph
	Experience	Has ridden for more than 1 year and rides more than 3 hours per week
Level 3	Distance	Can ride over 50 miles at a moderate intensity
	Time	Is comfortable with more than 2 hours on a ride
	Speed	Comfortable speed is 16–18 mph
	Experience	Rides about 2,500 miles per year or 300+ miles a month
Level 4	Distance	Enjoys the long rides over 50 miles at a moderate to hard intensity
	Time	Is comfortable with more than 4 hours on some rides
	Speed	Comfortable speed is more than 18 mph
	Experience	Rides about 3,500 to 4,000 miles per year or 400+ miles a month
Level 5	Distance	Enjoys the long rides over 75 miles at a moderate to hard intensity
	Time	Is comfortable with more than 5 hours on some rides
	Speed	Comfortable speed is more than 20 mph
	Experience	Rides about 4,500 to 6,000 miles per year or 500+ miles a month

combination, recovery, or assessment), percentage of maximum or threshold heart rate, how long the ride takes, and an approximation of Heart Zones Training Points (training load). The information in the Ride Selection Criteria section of the ride corresponds to the Heart Zones Ride Selection Criteria Chart (see Table 8.5, also located in Appendix B).

The Set by Rider's Fitness Level helps you select the appropriate intensities for your fitness level along with work and recovery interval times, number of sets or repeats, cadence ranges, and all the other information pertinent to the main set of the ride. You simply select your fitness level and follow the column down for your main set prescription. If you are unsure of your fitness level, refer again to Table 8.6.

Next you will find the Rider's Notes, along with a heart rate profile of the ride. The Rider's Notes give a quick step-by-step guide to the ride, and the heart rate profile lets you see at a glance the variation in heart rate zones built into the ride.

Finally, the Ride Overview provides a narrative about the ride, expanding on the purpose, overall "feel" of the ride, and suggested terrain.

THE HEART ZONES LIBRARY OF RIDES

This book gives you a catalog of more than thirty different rides and assessments. Want more? These rides are just the beginning! On the Heart Zones Web site, www.heartzones.com, we are building more than a catalog; we are building a *library* of rides, and we want your help. In this online library, you will be able to look up rides by type, intensity, terrain, and more. The most exciting aspect of this library is that the entire Heart Zones Cycling community is able to submit rides to the library, so the number of rides available to you will be enormous. You will never ride the same again!

WRITE YOUR OWN RIDES

We encourage you to create your own rides and e-mail or fax them to us. We will give them a try and give you feedback. We welcome your participation in growing the Library of Rides. All of our contact information is on the Web at www.HeartZones.com; or e-mail us at staff@heartzones.com.

PUTTING IT ALL TOGETHER: A SAMPLE RIDE PLAN

Periodizing your training program by distributing and sequencing your training load is essential for improvement. The four different ride types—steady state, interval, recovery, and combination—provide the variation in training load that you need and are the daily workouts for each of the training blocks (Preparation 1 and Preparation 2, Competition, and Transition).

The following sample ride plan is just that—only a sample. It is for a specific rider on a specific branch of the Training Tree, with a specific range of training load, for a specific ride goal, for a specific period of time inside a specific macrocycle. Your training plan will look similar, but with different rides, different ride types, and different intensities that are right for you at the right time in the right sequence.

Janice is an event rider (an "advanced beginner") who is using threshold heart rate to anchor her zones. She is developing a ride plan for the Preparation 1 and Preparation 2 mesocycles. Janice has decided to work on her base for eight weeks. The Threshold Heart Rate Training Tree tells her that for the weeks she is working in the Base branch, her distribution of time in the zones should be like that shown in Table 8.7.

TABLE 8.7 Time in Zones for Base Branch of Preparation 1

	Aerobic				Threshold	Nonaerobic		
Zones	1	2	3	4	T	5a	5b	5c
Time distribution	20%	40%	30%	10%				

Janice has a time budget of about 300 minutes a week (2,400 minutes for the eight weeks). She figures out her time in each zone for the eight weeks, based on her Training Tree and her time budget:

Zone 1: 480 minutes (20 percent of 2,400 minutes)

Zone 2: 960 minutes (40 percent of 2,400 minutes)

Zone 3: 720 minutes (30 percent of 2,400 minutes)

Zone 4: 240 minutes (10 percent of 2,400 minutes)

Using the training load formula (Load = Intensity × Volume of Time) to calculate training load, she figures out that her total training load for the four weeks should be the following:

$$(1 \times 480) + (2 \times 960) + (3 \times 720) + (4 \times 240) = 5,520 \text{ training points}$$

That averages out to about 690 training points each week, which is a "low to moderate" training load for her—right where it should be for the Base branch. She can now select rides that will average about 690 training points from about 300 minutes of riding time each week.

So far, so good. She begins to narrow down the list of rides that might work for her during this particular eight-week period. First, she looks at the Rides by Training Block (see Table 8.1, which can also be found in Appendix B). Because the Base branch of the Training Tree is in the Preparation 1 mesocycle, she looks for rides that are indicated for Preparation 1 and finds thirteen of them:

1 Cadence Drills and Skills

2 Crisscross Zone 2

3 Crisscross Zone 3

4 Rock Steady

5 Easy Rider 1

6 Easy Rider 2

7 Easy Rider 3

8 Turtle Rock

9 Pyramid Scheme 1

10 Steady State Ride

11 Fix It

12 Recovery Interval

13 Comin' Round the Mountain

Next, she looks at each ride in more detail, focusing on the sets for riders in fitness level 2, which is where she feels she is right now. Janice considers the range of training points available from each ride and selects a number to work with. Her plan for the first four weeks of her base training is shown in Table 8.8.

Moving along in her planning, Janice is thinking about her Strength branch, which is part of Preparation 2. The Threshold Heart Rate Training Tree tells her that for the two weeks she is working in the Strength branch, her distribution of time in the zones should resemble those shown in Table 8.9.

During these two weeks, she budgets about 700 minutes per week, or about 1,400 minutes. She figures out her time in each zone based on her Training Tree and her time budget:

Zone 1: 140 minutes (10 percent of 1,400 minutes)
Zone 2: 140 minutes (10 percent of 1,400 minutes)
Zone 3: 420 minutes (30 percent of 1,400 minutes)
Zone 4: 700 minutes (50 percent of 1,400 minutes)

Using the training load formula to calculate training load, Janice figures out that her total training load for the three weeks should break down as follows:

$$(1 \times 140) + (2 \times 140) + (3 \times 420) + (4 \times 700) = 4{,}480 \text{ training points}$$
(or 2,240 training points per week)

Just as before, Janice begins to narrow down the list of rides that might work for her during this particular training period. She looks at the Rides by Training Block Chart (Table 8.1; also located in Appendix B) and selects rides that are indicated for Preparation 2. A total of nineteen rides are listed for Preparation 2:

TABLE 8.8 Janice's Four-Week Base Branch Ride Plan

WEEK 1	Day 1	Day 2	Day 3	Day 4	Day 5	Day 6	Day 7	TOTAL
Low Intensity, Low Volume	Threshold or Maximum Testing* Set Zones	Rest Day*	Easy Rider 1*	Rest Day*	Easy Rider 2*	Rock Steady	Turtle Rock*	
TIME (MIN.)	75		45		45	60	60	285
HEART ZONES TRAINING POINTS	200		100		120	125	175	720

WEEK 2	Day 1	Day 2	Day 3	Day 4	Day 5	Day 6	Day 7	TOTAL
Low Intensity, Moderate Volume	Rest Day	Aerobic Time Trial	Crisscross 2	Easy Rider 1	Rest Day	Turtle Rock*	Rock Steady	
TIME (MIN.)		60	60	60		60	75	315
HEART ZONES TRAINING POINTS		180	120	120		150	150	720

WEEK 3	Day 1	Day 2	Day 3	Day 4	Day 5	Day 6	Day 7	TOTAL
Low Intensity, High Volume	Rest Day	Steady State Ride*	Easy Rider 3	Cadence Drills Intensity: <75% M <85% T	Crisscross 3 Intensity: ~65%–75% M ~75%–85% T	Pyramid Scheme 1	Rest Day*	
TIME (MIN.)		90	60	60	60	100		370
HEART ZONES TRAINING POINTS		200	175	175	175	175		900

WEEK 4	Day 1	Day 2	Day 3	Day 4	Day 5	Day 6	Day 7	TOTAL
Low Intensity, Low Volume	Rest Day	Rest Day**	Recovery Interval Ride Intensity: <75% M <85% T	Easy Rider 1	Easy Rider 2	Crisscross 3 Intensity: <75% M <85% T	Group Ride or Rock Steady** Intensity: <75% M <85% T	
TIME (MIN.)			50	60	60	60	90	320
HEART ZONES TRAINING POINTS			120	120	140	175	150	705

*Take your resting heart rate on these days, before getting out of bed. If resting heart rate is 5–10 bpm higher than normal, take a rest day or do a recovery ride.

**Take your delta heart rate on these days. If delta heart rate is more than 30 bpm, take a rest day or do a recovery ride.

TABLE 8.9 Time in Zones for Strength Branch of Preparation 2

	Aerobic				Threshold	Nonaerobic		
Zones	1	2	3	4	T	5a	5b	5c
Time distribution	10%	10%	30%	50%				

1 Cadence Drills and Skills

2 Comin' Round the Mountain

3 Pyramid Scheme 2

4 Turtle Rock

5 Cruisin'

6 Easy Rider 2

7 Easy Rider 3

8 Galactic

9 Head for the Hills

10 Holy Smokes

11 Kowabunga

12 Rock Steady

13 Copy Cat

14 Sign Here, Press Hard

15 Silver Streak

16 Crisscross Zone 4

17 Hiccup

18 Fix It

19 Recovery Interval

After looking at each of the rides in detail, she selects the rides shown in Table 8.10 for her two-week Strength branch. After selecting a ride for the day, Janice will spend some time figuring out how to make the ride work for her to arrive at an appropriate number of training points for that day.

That's all there is to the planning process. Follow all the steps in the program, study the details of each ride, and select the rides appropriate for your physiological goals as directed by each branch of your Training Tree. At the end of each ride, each week, and each training block, assess your progress, review your plan, and update your log. Analyze your results, listen to your heart, and adjust your plan as needed.

See you at the finish line!

TABLE 8.11 Janice's Two-Week Strength Branch Ride Plan

WEEK 9	Day 1	Day 2	Day 3	Day 4	Day 5	Day 6	Day 7	TOTAL
Moderate Intensity, High Volume	Rest Day*	Crisscross Zone 4	Comin' Round the Mountain	Rest Day or Easy Rider 2	Kowabunga	Turtle Rock	Group Ride or Silver Streak*	
TIME (MIN.)		90	90	90	120	90	150	630
HEART ZONES TRAINING POINTS		250	170	150	350	225	400	1,545

WEEK 10	Day 1	Day 2	Day 3	Day 4	Day 5	Day 6	Day 7	TOTAL
Moderate Intensity, High Volume	Rest Day	Fix It	Pyramid Scheme 2	Cruisin'	Rest Day or Crisscross Zone 3	Rock Steady	Group Ride or Blowout*	
TIME (MIN.)		90	100	120	90	120	180	700
HEART ZONES TRAINING POINTS		225	210	250	220	350	425	1,680

*Take your resting heart rate on these days, before getting out of bed. If resting heart rate is 5–10 bpm higher than normal, take a rest day or do a recovery ride.

9

WRITE YOUR NEW STORY

Together, we have come a long way. In the previous eight chapters, you have learned how to get fitter, go faster, and ride farther. We know it is hard to change from the old to the new, but it is truly possible and well worth the effort.

As Eckhart Tolle, transformational expert and author of *The Power of Now*, explains, each of us lives out the story of his or her ego—in this case, his or her riding ego. The ego's storyline is repeated over and over, and as time goes on, we run the risk of having our lives determined by the needs of our stories rather than by who we are deep down inside.

What was your story eight chapters ago? Were you fast but could not sprint at the end, so you could never move up in the standings or make it to the podium? Or maybe you could ride fifty miles but you just couldn't find the motivation to do a century. Most of us believe our old story and want to stay with it; it's buried deep in us, and it's hard to dislodge the roots that keep us firmly stuck there. But if there is a better way, why not give it a shot?

Give the new way a strong effort—you are going to see results. If you keep riding the same old way, you know what the results are:

possibly slight improvement. If, on the other hand, you take the risk of riding with your heart, your zones, your seven-step program, the methodology with you as the center of the framework, then you are in a whole new game. You are going to ride faster, ride farther, and finish well in events that you once thought were impossible for you. Everyone who uses this training methodology has experienced success. Why not you?

You are going to enjoy riding even more, see better results, and have renewed enthusiasm and motivation to ride. The benefits from putting in the miles riding the new way are so powerful that your storyline, your defense of your ego, changes. You might even discover that you are telling your riding partners, supporters, and friends that you have discovered a "new way of riding" that has changed how you ride. You do not have to buy a new bike, you do not have to go to a camp for a month, and you do not have to change your diet. All you have to do is apply the new step-by-step approach, and you get to write a new story:

- as a new smart rider who incorporates the latest in riding systems to do better
- as a new competitive rider with faster splits and competition times
- as a new event rider who can ride terrains and stay with other riders you could not hang with before
- as a new "power tool" rider who uses the latest in technology to enhance your performance
- as a new motivated rider who eagerly looks forward to each phase of training
- as a new systematic rider who trains by using your threshold or maximum heart rate
- as a new performance rider who gets better on the bike with each workout
- as a new scientific rider who uses the latest in applied exercise science
- as a new assessment rider who uses tests to quantify your improvement

■ as a new rider that the other riders talk about because they think you must have a secret weapon, a new energy drink, or an expert coach

PIONEERING THE NEW CYCLING FRONTIER

In many ways, you are a pioneer, a homesteader in new cycling territory. As you learn this new way of riding, you may feel like a stranger in a strange land, at least at first. After all, you are a member of the first generation of riders using new technology in new ways to get better on the bike. These riders are the early adopters, the ones who are willing to take the risk of being out there in advance of the masses and willing to hold the leadership position against the majority who are riding the old way. You may hear the old regime criticize your new way and attack your new framework. When you meet resistance from the Old Guard riders, practice these do's and don'ts:

■ Don't get frustrated.

■ Don't quit.

■ Don't give in.

■ Don't say, "If I don't get results the first time, I'm out of here!"

■ Don't let the gravitational pull of the old way seduce you back.

■ Do teach.

■ Do show.

■ Do use yourself as an example.

■ Do share what you are doing and learning.

■ Do explain why this way is different and important.

■ Do loan them the new tools—the meters and the monitors—to see for themselves.

■ Do tell them how to try the new way.

■ Do give them a little space on your new real estate—the winner's podium.

■ Do give credit for your success where credit is due—to you, the new rider.

THE PAYOFF

We first spoke of entrainment way back in Chapter 1. Entrainment is that state of being when you and your bike are in total sync. Entrainment happens when you, the road, your level of cardiovascular fitness, your monitor's information, your energy, and the moment all come together and riding is effortless, free, and painless, and you feel as if you could ride forever. Entrainment can happen during high-intensity training rides or when you peak a big hill or when you feel awed by an amazingly beautiful vista stretching before you.

Many payoffs come from riding in the zones. The biggest of all is to achieve your big goal, the Big Kahuna. That is the ultimate entrainment moment. That is what training for performance is all about—achieving the goals that you set in Chapter 3, the big ones and the little ones. When I, Sally Edwards, competed in RAAM, Race Across America, starting in California and finishing in South Carolina, entrainment occurred many times for our team, Team Judy Flannery. Two months before the start of the race, I was called by a team member and asked to take the place of Judy Flannery in her honor. Judy was killed while training for the race, struck down by an underage driver who took the wheel for his drunken father. Judy was a mom with four kids and a role model in her Colorado community. When our team crossed that finish line 3,200 miles and seven days later in first place in our division, we were entrained with each other and with accomplishing the goal—to honor the memory of Judy, to make her proud of us, to feel her as if she were riding with us across America. That was our big payoff. There is just as big a payoff for you.

RAISE THE BAR

One of the last steps in succeeding at Heart Zones Cycling is to finish by raising the bar. That is, every time you finish an event or performance or competition, look at that performance as new information to gauge how high to raise the bar. You can compare yourself with others, or, even better, you can compare yourself with *yourself*. You can analyze your performance in terms of what you expected and what actually happened. You can look at the data that are now abundantly available to you by using your meters and monitors. You can use your heart rate monitor, power meter, DASH! GPS tool, and metabolic analyzers to gather additional physiological data to assess changes in your performance capacity.

Raising the bar is motivational. It keeps you in the game, on the bike, and riding to your peak performance. Raising the bar is what drives you around that cycling track we mentioned in Chapter 1 (see Figure 9.1). You go around and around, getting faster and riding farther with each circuit around the track. How about one more ride around the track before you dive into the rides in the next chapter?

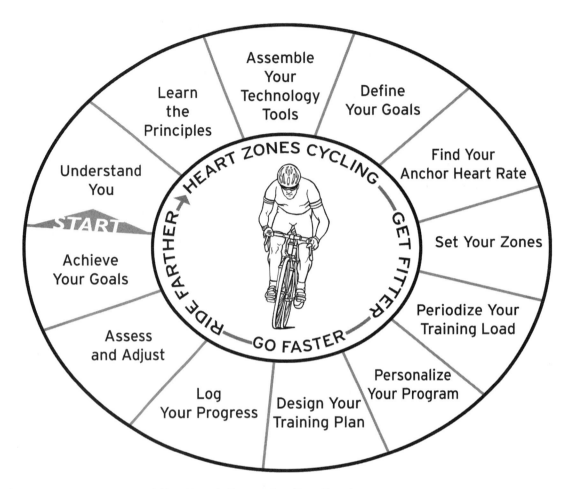

FIGURE 9.1 Around the Heart Zones Cycling Track

10

LEARN THE LINGO

This is it! You have your tools, your goals, your anchor heart rate, your zones, and your periodization plan. Now all you need to do is select rides that will give you the amount of training load you need and that focus on the physiological aims of your current branch of the Training Tree.

Well, almost. First, in this chapter you'll learn some commonly used terms that will help you interpret the details of each ride described in Appendix A (see the Glossary, as well). Second, as we mentioned in Chapter 8, several tools that might help you select rides are in Appendix B, too, including the following tables:

- Rides by Training Block
- Ride-O-Gram
- Five Fitness Levels of Riders
- Ride Selection Criteria

TRAINING DEFINITIONS

Aerobic endurance: This training develops the aerobic system and the cycling-specific muscles. It requires time in the saddle at a low intensity (Zones 1 and 2). The length of the endurance sessions will depend on the race or ride goal and the age and fitness level of the rider. Training for an endurance race or ride can mean training sessions at the same duration or up to 115 percent of the ride or race distance goal. Some riders may have training sessions up to 50 percent longer than the race time. The Preparation period of training consists primarily of this type of training.

Climbing accelerations: Accelerations or surges in cadence are performed during moderate (4 to 5 percent) prolonged climbs (10 to 30 minutes). The acceleration must be intense and usually lasts a minute or less with recovery into Zone 2 followed by another acceleration. These cadence surges help develop and clear lactate while under a high resistance (climbing).

Endurance race simulation: The purpose of this ride is to ride at a high intensity when you're in a fatigued state. It is done in the last 45 minutes of an endurance ride and is followed by a 20-minute warm-down. Maintaining appropriate cadence is key to getting the full benefit out of this training.

Hill sprints: These are short, high-intensity uphill sprints that develop muscular strength and nonaerobic power.

Long intervals: Interval training is often described as on/off training where the work or active part of the interval is considered "on," and the recovery part of the interval is considered "off." The ratio of the work/recovery or the on/off interval depends on your physiological goal. Long intervals are typically more than one minute. Recovery can be either active or static.

Muscular strength/endurance: The purpose of this training is to develop the nonfatiguing cycling-specific muscles; it is often referred to as *muscle tension*. It produces high tension in the fast-twitch muscle fibers and aids in the recruitment of fast oxidative glycolytic fibers.

Nonaerobic power: This training helps establish a high power output. It assists in the tolerance and buffering of lactic acid and efficiently utilizes it as an additional energy source.

PC jumps: This training increases ATP-PC output, which is the stored immediate source of energy for high-speed bursts or high-resistance movements lasting up to eight seconds.

Power starts: This training increases muscular strength and high power output. Intervals are short (15 seconds), starting at a very slow speed in a large gear and building quickly.

Recovery: Riding for shorter periods in Zones 1 and 2 can serve as recovery or warm-up and cool-down sessions. This low-intensity training is sometimes called *active recovery*.

Short intervals: Training sets consisting of alternating work and recovery intervals in which the work intervals are typically less than one minute and usually at a high intensity or all-out effort.

Sprints: Sprint training provides high-speed rhythm and coordination during maximal efforts such as a sprint to the finish line. They are short, all-out efforts.

Tempo: A large volume of training can be performed at this intensity, typically in Zone 3. Tempo training increases the aerobic capacity and efficiency by enhancing capillary density and oxidative enzymes.

Threshold: Threshold training is done at or around your threshold heart rate. *Threshold* is the intensity at which lactic acid begins to accumulate in your muscle cells as you cross from aerobic to non-oxidative efforts. It is the point at which, for general purposes, you go from using your aerobic system for energy to using primarily your nonaerobic system for energy. Your Threshold Cycling Test heart rate is usually higher than your lactate threshold heart rate because of the length of the test (10 minutes). If the test was twenty to thirty minutes, the heart rate values would correspond very closely. The purpose of this training is to raise your threshold, develop power, and improve your lactate clearance or buffering systems. This will also increase your steady state workload ability.

VO$_2$:   This training expands VO$_2$ capacity, thereby increasing the rate of oxygen delivery to the muscles. Well-trained endurance athletes typically have a high VO$_2$max. Typically for endurance cyclists, the higher the VO$_2$max, the better the performance.

GET ON THE BIKE!

Now it's time to get on your bike. Turn to Appendix A and you will find a catalog of rides we have created for you to use in your ride plan. In addition, there are a number of assessment rides to help you track your progress. Remember, assessing and adjusting are crucial steps in your training program.

GLOSSARY

Adaptation: The process of physiological change that occurs when the body responds to the stresses of training loads.

Aerobic: With or in the presence of oxygen; an exercise characterized by low-intensity activity.

Aerobic capacity: The largest volume of oxygen that your body can consume in one minute; also called maximal oxygen uptake, or VO_2max.

Aerobic energy system: Cellular respiration, in which carbohydrates are metabolized in the presence of oxygen to produce energy for the cell.

Aerobic fitness: The ability of the body to maintain exercise intensity while producing energy mainly from aerobic metabolism.

Aerobic metabolism: A process of energy production in which carbohydrates, fats, and proteins are used together to produce aerobic energy.

Aerodynamic: Streamlined; reduced air resistance.

Ambient heart rate: The number of beats per minute your heart contracts when you are awake but in a sedentary, stationary, or sitting position.

Anaerobic energy system: Metabolic process (glycolysis) in the absence of oxygen in which glucose is converted to lactic acid; this system provides energy for high-intensity activity and bridges gaps in energy when the aerobic energy system is fatigued.

Anaerobic metabolism: Oxidation (burning) on the cellular level primarily of carbohydrates without the ready availability of oxygen.

Anticipatory heart rate: The cardiac response from excitability, such as waiting for an event to start.

ATP-CP energy system: An anaerobic energy system in which ATP is manufactured when phosphocreatine (PC) is broken down. This system represents the most rapidly available source of ATP for use by muscle. Activities performed at maximum intensity in a period of 10 seconds or less derive energy (ATP) from this system.

Attack: An aggressive high-speed jump away from other riders.

Average heart rate: Average of all of the beats per minute during a period of time.

Base: A training term for the fitness level required to exercise for a relatively extended duration without tiring. Also the first branch on the Training Tree.

Blood glucose: Sugar in the bloodstream.

Blow up: To go out too fast and not be able to continue.

Bonk: To run out of energy.

Bottom (of a zone): The floor or lower limit of a Heart Zone.

Cadence: The number of revolutions per minute (rpm) that you spin.

Carbohydrates (CHO): Starches; sugars. Organic compounds that when broken down become a main energy source for muscular work. A chemical compound containing carbon, hydrogen, and oxygen.

Cardiac: Pertaining to the heart.

Cardiac cycle: The period of time between two consecutive heartbeats.

Cardiac drift: The rise in heart rate during exercise that occurs as a result of loss of blood volume principally from dehydration. Also known as *cardiovascular drift*.

Cardiac output: The amount or volume of blood pumped by the heart per minute. Cardiac output is the product of heart rate times stroke volume.

Cardiorespiratory: Pertaining to the circulatory and respiratory systems.

Ceiling: The top of a Heart Zone.

Crossover point: Threshold heart rate; the heart rate point when your metabolism shifts fuel sources from primarily burning fats to primarily burning carbohydrates.

Delta heart rate: The measurement of the difference between your heart rate lying down and your heart rate standing up.

Drafting: "Sitting in" or "tucking in"; riding behind others in their slipstream; this enables the second rider to maintain speed with less effort.

Duration: Length of time.

Economy: The oxygen consumption required for a given effort. Improved economy results in faster speeds at lower energy costs.

Electrolyte: A substance that ionizes in solution, such as table salt (NaCl), that is capable of conducting an electrical current; essential for cellular metabolism.

Emotional fitness: Ability to deal with stress, build positive relationships, deal with change, and maintain a positive mental attitude.

Endurance: The ability to exercise vigorously at a sustained rate for a period of time.

Endurance training: Also called *aerobic training*. A form of conditioning designed to increase aerobic capacity and hence endurance performance.

Endorphins: Natural chemicals similar to opiates released into the bloodstream by the brain that result in the feeling of happiness from training.

Energy: The capacity or ability to perform work.

Energy equation: Energy balance; the simple "energy in = energy out" equation also known as the first law of thermodynamics.

Energy shifting: A nondiet active approach to balancing eating with metabolic, emotional, and physical fitness.

Energy system: Any of the metabolic systems that each use different sources of energy (e.g., oxygen, phosphate, or lactate) to provide fuel for working muscles.

Exercise heart rate: The number of beats per minute you are experiencing during a workout.

Fartlek: A Scandinavian term meaning "speed-play." Rides of mixed terrain at varied intervals; unstructured intervals.

Fat: (1) Lipid; concentrated sources of energy for muscular work. They are compounds containing glycerol and fatty acids and may be saturated or unsaturated. (2) The soft tissue in the body other than that making up the skeletal muscle mass and the soft tissues.

Fat burning: Fat oxidation for energy production.

Fatigue: A state of weariness, discomfort, and decreased efficiency resulting from prolonged or excessive exertion.

First ventilatory threshold: VT_1; nonaerobic threshold. (1) The point at which your body is expiring more respiratory carbon dioxide than the quantity of inspired oxygen or the crossover point between aerobic and nonaerobic exercise. (2) The intensity-dependent "shift" in the metabolic pathways that supply energy for work. The point at which the body switches from primarily oxidative energy-producing pathways to increased anaerobic-glycolytic energy-producing pathways.

Flexibility: The range of motion about a joint; two types: static flexibility or dynamic flexibility.

Floor: The bottom of a Heart Zone.

Free fatty acid (FFA): The usable form of triglycerides.

Frequency: How often an exercise activity is done in a given amount of time.

Functional capacity: The ability to do normal daily activities, especially work. Also known as *fitness capacity*.

Gas analyzer: Metabolic assessment cart; a device that measures the volume, concentration, and content of inspired and expired atmospheric air.

Grade Exercise Test: A fitness assessment test that uses progressively higher work intensities throughout the test. Also known as a *stress test*.

Glucose: Sugar; $C_6H_{12}O_6$.

Glycogen: A polymer of glucose stored in the body.

Glycogen loading: Supercompensation; an exercise-diet procedure that elevates muscle glycogen stores to concentrations two to three times normal.

Glycogen sparing: The diminished utilization of glycogen that results when other fuels available are used for activity.

Glycolysis: The incomplete chemical breakdown of carbohydrate. The anaerobic reactions in this breakdown release energy for the manufacture of ATP as they produce lactic acid. Anaerobic glycolysis is also known as the *lactic acid system*.

Hammer: Hard, sustained effort.

Heart rate point: A single heart rate number that is a marker such as midpoint or threshold heart rate point.

Heart Zones Training: A methodology of training that uses the heart, zones, and exercise goals to achieve optimum results. The methodology uses training technologies such as heart rate monitors, GPS monitors, power meters, accelerometers, and metabolic analyzers.

Hypoglycemia: Low blood sugar level. (Contrast: *Hyper*glycemia is high blood sugar levels.)

Intensity: The degree of energy or effort, as related to a workout.

Interval: The duration of a given intensity of training. Used in training to mean a set of stress and recovery sessions.

Interval training: An exercise type in which there is a series of short but regularly repeated periods of work stress interspersed with adequate periods of rest or relief.

Isolated leg training (ILT): Training technique of pedaling with one leg to improve performance.

Jam: A high-speed riding or an extended chase.

Jump: A burst of speed.

Kick: A final burst of speed.

Kilocalorie (calorie): A unit of work or energy equal to the amount of heat required to raise the temperature of one kilogram of water 1 degree Centigrade.

Lactate analyzer: A monitoring device that measures blood lactate levels.

Lactate threshold (LT): (1) The point when the accumulation of lactate in the bloodstream increases rapidly above the 2.0 level as the result of increases in exercise intensity. (2) Work intensity, often expressed as a percentage of maximum oxygen uptake or a corresponding heart rate, at which a maximum lactate steady state is reached; determined by analyzing lactate samples from an incremental exercise test.

Lactic acid: Product of the body's metabolic processes that is created in all of the heart rate zones and is shuttled away from the skeletal muscles to different parts of the body where it is oxidized.

Leg speed: How fast you can turn the cranks.

Load: The amount of stress on the system. In the Heart Zones methodology, load is calculated by multiplying time in the zone by the "weight" or intensity factor of the zone. There are three types of load: metabolic, emotional, and physical.

Mash: To push a big gear or push down on the pedals.

Maximum accumulated oxygen deficit (MAOD): Oxygen deficit; the difference between the oxygen equivalent of the work performed and the oxygen consumed during a nonaerobic capacity test. An estimation of nonaerobic or nonoxidative capacity.

Maximum heart rate: The highest number of cardiac contractions or beats in one minute at maximal exertion.

Maximal lactate steady state (max LaSS): The maximum work intensity that will not cause a continual increase in blood lactate levels after the initial warm-up period.

Metabolic (VO$_2$) Test: An assessment that measures the rate and type of caloric consumption (EE or energy expenditure) using oxygen measurements.

Metabolism: The sum of all the chemical processes in the body resulting in energy production and growth.

Midpoint heart rate: The heart rate number that is in the middle of a heart zone.

Minimum heart rate: The lowest recorded heart rate during the activity.

Mitochondria: Intracellular structures that carry out cellular respiration.

Model: A type of training program that serves as an example.

Muscular endurance: The ability of a muscle or muscle group to perform repeated contractions for a long period of time while bearing a load.

Neuromuscular: Related to nerves and muscles.

New Fitness: The practice of exercise training based on sound interpretation of current exercise physiology research.

Nutrition: The process of assimilating food.

Off the back: "Dropped"; describes one or more riders who have failed to keep pace with the peloton or group.

Overload: To exercise a muscle or muscle group against resistance greater than that which is normally encountered. The resistance or load can be maximal or submaximal.

Overreaching: Training that results in negative muscle fatigue; short-term training to exhaustion of the body's adaptivity.

Overtraining: Training too hard to the point of imbalance from too much stress with too little time for regeneration. Also referred to as *misadaptation* or *underrecovery*.

Oxygen consumption: The intake and utilization of oxygen by the body.

Oxygen uptake (VO$_2$): The volume of oxygen uptake or the capacity of the heart and lungs to supply oxygen to working tissues.

Paceline: A group of riders in a line, alternating turns pulling at the front and sitting in, or drafting, behind others.

Pairing: When a sending device and a receiving device connect and communicate with each other. Heart rate monitor transmitters and receivers pair when they make a connection.

Palpate: To apply touch, as in palpating an artery in order to manually count heart rate.

Peak heart rate: The highest heart rate during any one workout period.

Peak power: Highest power output in any one workout, typically measured in short, high-intensity sprint tests and measured in watts or watts per kilogram.

Peloton: Pack; field; bunch; the main group of riders.

Percentage of maximum heart rate: A relative heart rate number. The absolute heart rate number divided by maximum heart rate number.

Percentage of threshold heart rate: A relative heart rate number. The absolute heart rate number divided by threshold heart rate number.

Periodization: A method of training that alters the cycle of stress and recovery periods within a training sequence or block.

Pickups: A type of training that includes several quick bursts of speed.

Power: Work divided by time or the rate of doing work. Power combines a cyclist's strength (force on the pedals) and velocity (distance divided by time).

Profile: A heart rate graph of a session of activity.

Program: The application of a methodology in the context of a system, including a step-by-step progression of activities that leads to attaining a goal.

Protein: A basic food containing amino acids.

Pull: To take a turn at the front of a group of riders while maintaining the same pace.

Pull off: To move over and allow another rider to take the lead in a pull.

Pull through: To assume the lead and take the wind.

Quality: Matching the intensity in training with the goal of the workouts.

R > 1.0: Method of determining threshold that uses R (respiratory exchange ratio) exceeding 1.0 level.

Recovery: The time between intervals. There are two types: *total recovery*, in which the rider stops moving, and *active recovery*, in which the rider continues to move slowly. Recovery can also be *interrecovery*, achieving rest benefits by taking relief time between workout sessions, usually between workout days; and *intrarecovery*, a way of doing intervals such that recovery is within one workout session rather than between workouts.

Recovery heart rate: The difference in the heart rate after an exercise session and after rest and commonly measured one or two minutes after stopping or slowing exercise.

Repeats: Repetitions of the same work interval.

Respiratory exchange ratio (RER or R): The estimation of cellular respiratory quotient, and the proportion of lipid and carbohydrate being metabolized for energy. The formula is VCO_2/VO_2.

Respiratory quotient (RQ): At the cellular level, the ratio cellular respiration of carbon dioxide (CO_2) produced and oxygen (O_2) consumed; represents at the cellular level the ratio of CO_2/O_2.

Resting heart rate: The number of heart beats per minute when the body is at complete rest.

Riding: Cycling; time on the bike.

Road race: A race performed on paved surfaces; different from a track or a mountain bike race. Road races are divided specifically into criteriums, time trials, and road races. The specific road race is a mass start event over a course more than one mile long. Road races may be point-to-point or circuits.

Set: A group of repetitions of work and relief intervals.

Sharpening: Peaking; a limb near the top of the Training Tree. A period of training in which training load is highest.

Slipstream: The area of least wind resistance behind a rider; a place where a rider drafts as "in the slipstream."

Specificity: A way of training that stresses the muscle groups and energy systems to meet the demands of the event or activity.

Speed: Quickness; how fast you can go.

Spin: To pedal at a high cadence.

Spin out: To be unable to increase cadence, spinning as fast as possible. May imply the need for a bigger gear.

Spinner: A rider who maintains a high cadence in a moderate gear.

Spinning: Pedaling at a high frequency, cadence, or revolutions per minute.

Sprint: Acceleration to speed.

Steady state: A heart rate or training rate that is submaximal and maintained at a constant intensity, speed, or rate of work.

Strength: The maximum force or tension that a muscle can produce against resistance.

Stress test: Assessment done while exercising during which fitness and health care professionals measure physiological responses using sophisticated gas exchange and EMG devices.

Stroke Volume: The amount of blood pumped by the ventricles of the heart per beat.

Submaximal: Exercise intensities below VO_2max.

Substrate utilization: The fuels that are oxidized or burned during a period of time.

Supramaximal: Exercise intensities greater than VO_2max.

Technique: Biomotor skills.

Tempo: Steady pace.

Tempo training: Continuous training with no interrecovery; tempo training is usually done below 80 percent of maximum heart rate or ~90 percent of threshold heart rate.

Threshold heart rate: The heart rate at the crossover point between aerobic and nonaerobic exercise.

Threshold training: Training that improves the efficiency of the anaerobic energy-producing systems and can increase muscular strength and tolerance for acid-base imbalances during high-intensity effort.

Time in zone (TIZ): The sum of all time within a single Heart Zone.

Time trial: A way of training or racing over a fixed distance to assess how long it takes the rider to complete the course.

Training: (1) A program of physical activity designed to improve the skills and fitness capacities of an individual. (2) Any sustained exercise—cardiovascular, resistance, or combinations—done at a heart rate or intensity level sufficient to result in metabolic adaptation in the muscles or systems involved.

Training effect: The physiological benefits of a given workout or ride.

Training framework: A training program that includes all aspects of the whole athlete. The training framework is a global picture, the structure that frames the rider.

Training load: The measurement of the amount of physical stress that you are experiencing. There are different types of training load, such as external training load and internal training load. Measurement of training load is essential for proper training. External training load is the product of distance or time (volume) and intensity, frequency, and mode.

Training methodology: How you train; the approach or method that is used to set up the training program built on principles that form the foundation. For example, Heart Zones Training is a methodology built on twelve principles of training.

Training plan: The road map and the ride schedule fused together into a document that provides you with a schedule of training.

Training program: How you put together the rides into a step-by-step method.

Training structure: The framework of a training methodology.

Training system: The way the training methodology is executed, as defined by physiological anchor points, such as maximum heart rate or threshold heart rate.

Transceiver: A transceiver is a combination transmitter/receiver in a single device.

Triglycerides: The chemical name for the fat stored in the body; the stored form of free fatty acids.

Variability training: Varying workouts so they provide the stimulus-response training effect. The opposite of "monotony training."

VDOT: Velocity at your VO_2max; created by Jack Daniels.

Ventilatory equivalent (VE): The amount of total inspired air per minute.

Ventilatory threshold (VT): Work intensity, often expressed as a percentage of maximum oxygen uptake or a corresponding heart rate, at which a maximum lactate steady state is reached; determined through the use of ventilatory gas measures. It is commonly thought that there are two different ventilatory thresholds.

vVO_2: Velocity at maximum aerobic capacity or VO_2.

VO_2max: Your maximum aerobic capacity or maximum oxygen consumption capacity. This is a quantitative measurement expressed in milliliters of oxygen consumed per kilogram of body weight per minute (ml/kg/min.). It is synonymous with *maximum oxygen consumption*. See *aerobic capacity*.

VO_2max heart rate: The number of beats per minute at your aerobic capacity. Your heart rate at VDOT.

Volume: The amount of training time or distance, usually expressed in one week's period of time.

Volume of carbon dioxide (VCO_2): Volume of carbon dioxide expired or minute volume of expired carbon dioxide.

Waypoint: A navigation fix. Usually a destination or point of reference.

Wind up: To accelerate up to speed.

Work: Application of a force through a distance.

Work intervals: The portion of an interval training program consisting of the stress or the work effort.

Workload: Total training volume as measured by training frequency, intensity, and duration.

Work-recovery ratio: The relative proportions of work and recovery; in interval training, the ratio of the duration of the work effort or interval to the duration of the rest or recovery interval.

Workout types: What the rider does during a ride or workout. There are four different workout types: steady state, interval, recovery, and combinations.

Zone: A range of heartbeats.

Zone size: The dimensions of a heart zone. All heart zones have a size equal to 10 percent of the maximum heart rate in the max system. In the threshold training system, all zones are ~10 percent of threshold heart rate *below* threshold of ~5 percent above threshold.

Zone weight: The mathematical value representing intensity that is used to determine training load.

BIBLIOGRAPHY

American College of Sport Medicine. 2003. *ACSM Fitness Book, 3rd ed*. Champaign, IL: Human Kinetics.

Bandura, A., and D. Cervone. 1983. "Self-Evaluative and Self-Efficacy Mechanisms Governing the Motivational Effects of Goal Systems." *Journal of Personality and Social Psychology* 45:1017–28.

Bompa, Tudor. 1999. *Periodization: Theory and Methodology of Training*. Champaign, IL: Human Kinetics.

Borg, Gunmar. 1998. *Borg's Perceived Exertion and Pain Scales*. Champaign, IL: Human Kinetics.

Brown, Lorraine, and Sally Edwards. 2003. *Fit and Fat: An 8-Week Heart Zones Training Program*. New York: Alpha Books.

Burke, Ed. 2002. *Serious Cycling, 2nd ed*. Champaign, IL: Human Kinetics.

Dalai Lama. 1998. *The Art of Happiness*. New York: Riverhead Books.

Edwards, Sally. 1993. *The Heart Rate Monitor Book*. Sacramento, CA: Heart Zones Publishing.

———. 1996. *Heart Zone Training: Exercise Smart, Stay Fit, and Live Longer*. Avon, MA: Adams Media.

Edwards, Sally, and Sally Reed. 2002. *The Heart Rate Monitor Book for Cyclists*. Boulder, CO: VeloPress.

———. 2002. *The Heart Rate Monitor Workbook for Cyclists*. Boulder, CO: VeloPress.

Foster, Carl, and Peter J. Maud. 2006. *Physiological Assessments of Human Fitness*. Champaign, IL: Human Kinetics.

Friel, Joe. 2003. *The Cyclist's Training Bible, 3rd ed*. Boulder, CO: VeloPress.

Jeukendrup, Asker E. 2002. *High-Performance Cycling*. Champaign, IL: Human Kinetics.

Martin, David, and Sebastian Coe. 1997. *Better Training for Distance Runners, 2nd ed*. Champaign, IL: Human Kinetics.

Noakes, Tim. 2002. *Lore of Running*. 4th ed. Champaign, IL: Human Kinetics.

Olds, T. S., K. I. Norton, E. L. A. Lowe, et al. 1995. "Modeling Road Cycling Performance." *Journal of Applied Physiology* 78:1596–1611.

Robergs, Robert A., and Roberto Landwehr. 2002. "Prediction of Maximum Heart Rate." *Journal of Exercise Physiology* 5, no. 2.

Rudd, Dan, and Sally Edwards. 2004. *Health in a Heartbeat: A 6-Week Emotional Fitness Training Program*. Sacramento, CA: Heart Zones Publishing.

Tolle, Eckhart. 1999. *The Power of Now: A Guide to Spiritual Enlightenment*. Novato, CA: New World Library.

USA Cycling Coaching Staff and Coaching Education Staff. 2005. *2005 USA Cycling Expert Coach Manual*. Colorado Springs, CO: USA Cycling.

Wilmore, Jack, and David Costill. 1999. *Physiology of Sport and Exercise, Rev. ed*. Champaign, IL: Human Kinetics.

APPENDIX A:
THE RIDES

TRAINING RIDES

BLOWOUT

Ride Selection Criteria

Type	Combination
Purpose	Overall training with variations in intensity and cadence
Intensity	Aerobic, threshold, nonaerobic, ATP-PC
% Maximum HR	60%–90+%
% Threshold HR	~70%–105+%
Zones	2–5 (max HR); 2–5b (Threshold)
Mesocycle	Preparation 2, Competition
Terrain	Flat, rolling
Time	1.5–2.5 hours
Heart Zones Points	~280–400 (max HR); ~280–415 (Threshold)

Set(s) by Rider's Fitness Level

	Level 1[1]	Level 2	Level 3	Level 4	Level 5
Spin-Ups[2] Repeats	—	5	5	5	5
Spin-Ups Zones	—	2–3	2–3	2–3	2–3
Power Starts[3] Repeats		2	3	3	3
Power Starts Zones	—	2–4	2–4	2–4	2–4
Time Trial	—	3 min.	4 min.	6 min.	8 min.
% Maximum[4] HR	—	60%–80%	60%–90%	60%–90+%	60%–90+%
% Threshold HR	—	~70%–100%	~70%–105%	~70%–105+%	~70%–105+%
Pyramid[5]	—	See notes	See notes	See notes	See notes
PC Jumps[6]	—	See notes	See notes	See notes	See notes
All-Out Effort	—	8 sec.	8 sec.	8 sec.	8 sec.
Recovery for Time Trial	—	1 min.	1 min.	1.5 min.	2 min.
Work-Recovery Ratio	—	1:3	1:4	1:4	1:4

General Notes on Fitness Level Tables:

- This ride is not recommended for Level 1 riders.
- Spin-Ups—moderate gearing, building cadence from 60 rpm to 120 rpm in 60 seconds.
- Power Starts—designed to increase muscular strength and nonaerobic power. Start from a very slow speed in a large gear and build to high speed over 15 seconds.
- If you know your threshold heart rate number, use that number even if you are training using maximum heart rate zones.
- Pyramid—"hard" effort is threshold heart rate or higher
- PC Jumps—high-speed burst with high resistance, lasting up to eight seconds. Designed to increase ATP-PC output using the stored energy source in the muscles.

Heart Rate Profile and Rider's Notes

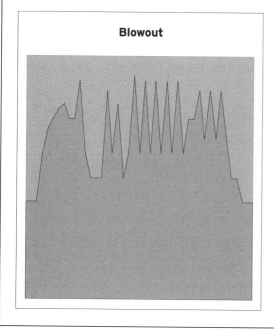

Blowout

1. Warm up 20–30 minutes.
2. Do five Spin-Ups from 60 rpm to 120 rpm. Moderate gearing.
3. Ride 10 minutes in Zone 3 (tempo riding), cadence 70–75 rpm.
4. Do two to three 15-second Power Starts with 5-minute recovery between repeats.
5. Ride your Time Trial time twice, cadence 80–95 rpm. Recover according to fitness level.
6. Pyramid—Zones 4–5:
   1 minute hard/1 minute recover
   2 minutes hard/2 minutes recover
   3 minutes hard/3 minutes recover
   4 minutes hard/4 minutes recover
7. Ride 10 minutes in Zone 3 (Tempo riding), cadence 70–75 rpm.
8. Choice: Do three PC Jumps of 8–10 seconds with 60-second recovery between repeats.
9. Cool down 20–30 minutes in Zone 2.

Ride Overview

This ride is a little bit like Fourth of July finale fireworks. It offers a variety of specialty training and should be done only after a strong aerobic base has been developed in Preparation 1 and 2 training.

Choose a course that is flat to rolling, and warm up for 20–30 minutes.

First on the agenda are Spin-Ups, which will work on smoothing out your pedal stroke and will gradually increase your heart rate in preparation for the tempo training. Tempo riding is done below 80 percent of maximum heart rate or ~90 percent of threshold heart rate. Cadence is 70–75 rpm.

Next are Power Starts done from a very slow roll with heavy resistance or big gearing. Build speed over 15 seconds; then recover for 5 minutes before repeating.

Next you will challenge yourself with two Time Trials, pushing your threshold higher and holding a steady cadence of 80–95 rpm. Recover between repeats according to your fitness level.

Find a nice flat road for the next challenge. The pyramid will help develop your muscular endurance and strength while improving your lactate threshold. Cadence will be 90–100 rpm. Stay steady and focused on your work intervals.

A 10-minute tempo ride follows that will help your legs and lungs recover before ending your ride with one last blowout.

If you still have some legs left, finish with up to three PC Jumps of 8–10 seconds each with a 60-second recovery between repeats. PC Jumps will help increase your ATP-PC output, which is energy stored in your legs for high-speed bursts with resistance.

Finish your ride with a 20–30-minute cool-down, and pat yourself on the back!

CADENCE SKILLS AND DRILLS

Ride Selection Criteria

Type	Interval
Purpose	Improve neuromuscular efficiency
Intensity	Aerobic
% Maximum HR	60%–80%
% Threshold HR	~70%–90%
Zones	2–4
Mesocycle	Preparation 1, Preparation 2
Terrain	Flat
Time	1–1.5 hours
Heart Zones Points	~150–190 (maximum and threshold)

Set(s) by Rider's Fitness Level

	Level 1	*Level 2*	*Level 3*	*Level 4*	*Level 5*
Number of Sets	1	1	1	1	1
% Maximum HR	60%–75%	60%–80%	60%–80%	60%–80%	60%–80%
% Threshold HR	~70%–85%	~70%–90%	~70%–90%	~70%–90%	~70%–90%

Heart Rate Profile and Rider's Notes

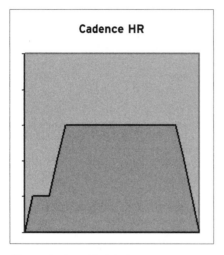

Cadence HR

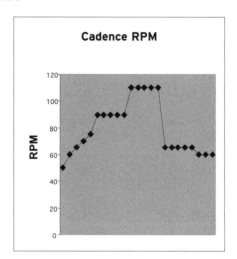

Cadence RPM

(Example: Level 3 rider)
 1. For 30 minutes, warm up to the bottom of Zone 2.
 2. For 5 minutes, increase cadence to 80–100 rpm and heart rate to the bottom of Zone 4.
 3. For 5 minutes, increase cadence to 110+ and hold heart rate at bottom of Zone 4.
 4. For 5 minutes, decrease cadence to 70 rpm and keep heart rate at bottom of Zone 4.
 5. Cool down for 15–30 minutes.

Note: For Preparation 1 training, keep all rate intensities under 75% of maximum or under ~85% of threshold.

Ride Overview

This is a great ride to do when you want to intersperse a little higher intensity into your Block 1 and Block 2 training and work on improving your pedal stroke. Most of this ride is done on flat terrain. Warm up for 30 minutes to the bottom of Zone 2. Increase your heart rate to the bottom of Zone 4 for 5 minutes at a cadence between 80 and 100 rpm. Hold your heart rate steady at the bottom of Zone 4 while increasing your cadence to 110+ rpm for another 5 minutes. Decrease your cadence to 70 rpm or less for the next 5 minutes, and continue to hold a steady state heart rate of the bottom of Zone 4. Finish the ride with a 15–30-minute cool-down.

COMIN' ROUND THE MOUNTAIN

Ride Selection Criteria

Type	Combination
Purpose	Aerobic endurance, cycling specific muscular strength
Intensity	Aerobic
Zones	2–3
% Maximum HR	65%–80%
% Threshold HR	~75%–90%
Mesocycle	Preparation 1 and 2, Competition
Terrain	Flat, rolling, and hills
Time	1.5–3 hours
Heart Zones Points	~170–525 (maximum and threshold)

Sets by Rider's Fitness Level

Tempo Set	*Level 1*	*Level 2*	*Level 3*	*Level 4*	*Level 5*
Number of Repeats	1	2	2	3	3
% Maximum HR	70%–75%	75%–80%	75%–80%	75%–80%	75%–80%
% Threshold HR	~80%–85%	~85%–90%	~85%–90%	~85%–90%	~85%–90%
Work Interval	10 min.	10 min.	15 min.	20 min.	25 min.
Recovery Interval	5 min.	5 min.	7 min.	10 min.	12 min.
Work-Recovery Ratio	2:1	2:1	2:1	2:1	2:1
Cadence	70–75 rpm	70–75 rpm	70–75 rpm	70–75 rpm	70–75 rpm

Muscular Strength (tension) Set	*Level 1*	*Level 2*	*Level 3*	*Level 4*	*Level 5*
Number of Repeats	2	3	4	5	5
% Maximum HR	65%–70%	70%–75%	70%–75%	70%–75%	70%–75%
% Threshold HR	~75%–80%	~80%–85%	~80%–85%	~80%–85%	~80%–85%
Work Interval	5 min.	5 min.	5 min.	5 min.	5 min.
Recovery Interval	5 min.	5 min.	5 min.	5 min.	5 min.
Work-Recovery Ratio	1:1	1:1	1:1	1:1	1:1
Cadence	50–60 rpm	50–60 rpm	50–60 rpm	50–60 rpm	50–60 rpm

Heart Rate Profile and Rider's Notes

Comin' Round the Mountain

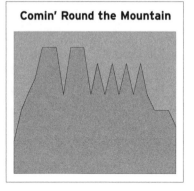

1. Warm up for 15–20 minutes.
2. Repeat tempo intervals according to fitness level. Cadence 70–75 rpm, moderately hard gearing.
3. Repeat muscular strength intervals according to fitness level. Cadence 50–60 rpm, gradual hill, big gear.
4. Cool down for 20–30 minutes.

Ride Overview

This combination ride includes tempo intervals designed to increase your aerobic efficiency and muscular strength (tension) intervals to develop cycling-specific strength. The tempo sets are done on flat to rolling hills near 80 percent of maximum heart rate or ~90 percent of threshold heart rate using moderately hard gearing and a cadence of 70–75 rpm. Head for the hills when you start your muscular strength intervals. Choose a moderate grade of 4 to 5 percent. Big gears are used to produce low cadence (50–60 rpm). It is important that you maintain correct form and remain in the saddle, stay relaxed, and keep your upper body quiet. Keep your heart rate moderate (70 to 75 percent of maximum or ~80 to 85 percent of threshold). Cool down for a minimum of 20–30 minutes.

COPY CAT

Ride Selection Criteria

Type	Combination
Purpose	Increase ability to ride at high intensity while in a fatigued state
Intensity	Aerobic, threshold, nonaerobic, ATP-PC
Zones	2–5 (maximum HR); 2–5b (threshold HR)
% Maximum HR	60%–90+%
% Threshold HR	~70%–105+%
Mesocycle	Preparation 2, Competition
Terrain	Varied
Time	1.5–4 hours
Heart Zones Points	~270–520 (maximum); ~270–550 (threshold)

Set(s) by Rider's Fitness Level

	Level 1	*Level 2*	*Level 3*	*Level 4*	*Level 5*
% Maximum HR	—	85%	85%–90%	90+%	90+%
% Threshold HR	—	~95%	~95%–100%	105+%	105+%
VO_2 Time Trial Flat	—	4 min.	6 min.	8 min.	8 min.
Recovery for Time Trial	—	3 min.	4 min.	6 min.	6 min.
VO_2 Hill Climb	—	2 min.	4 min.	6 min.	6 min.
Recovery for Hill Climb	—	1 min.	<2 min.	<3 min.	<3 min.
Sprint	—	10 sec.	12 sec.	15 sec.	15 sec.
Recovery between Sprints	—	5 min.	5 min.	5 min.	5 min.

Heart Rate Profile and Rider's Notes

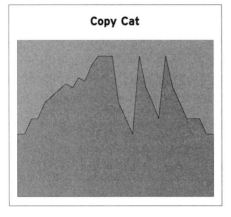

Copy Cat

(Example for Level 3)
1. Warm up for 15–20 minutes.
2. Endurance ride in Zone 3 at 80–95 rpm.
3. Do one Time Trial at VO_2 pace according to fitness level, or do two Hill Climbs at VO_2 pace according to fitness level.
4. Recover according to fitness level.
5. Ride one or two all-out 10–15-second Sprints with 5-minute recovery.
6. Cool down 20 minutes.

Note: Not recommended for Level 1 riders.

Ride Overview

Races vary not only in length but in terrain characteristics such as hills and corners. Environmental changes in temperature, humidity, and wind can also affect a race. The key is matching your fitness and skill level with the demands of the course. The longer the ride, the more aerobic endurance and cycling economy you will need, but you will still need muscular strength to deal with the hills. This ride will tell you what your strengths and weaknesses are so that you can improve to meet the demands of the event.

The purpose of this ride is to simulate a race situation where the body is fatigued and there are still 20 or 25 hard minutes left in the race. Choose varied terrain for this ride. The first part of the ride will be done at a lower intensity (Zones 2 and 3) and a cadence between 80 and 95 rpm. The length of the first part of the ride will depend on your fitness level and training goal. It can be anywhere from 90 minutes to 3 or 4 hours. The focus will be on what you do in the last 20–25 minutes of the ride.

Once you have completed the endurance part of your ride, the challenge will be to complete the next 20–25 minutes at high intensity.

If the road is flat to rolling:

■ Complete a 4–8-minute time trial according to your fitness level at VO_2 pace (90+% for maximum heart rate or 105+% for threshold heart rate). Recovery is 3–6 minutes.

■ Complete two all-out, 10–15-second sprints with 5 minutes of recovery in between.

■ Finish with a 20-minute cool-down.

If the road is hilly:

■ Climb between 2 and 6 minutes, according to your fitness level, at VO_2 intensity, using the downhill as recovery. Recovery should be half the active time. Repeat.

■ Complete one all-out, 10–15-second sprint.

■ Finish with a 20-minute cool-down.

CRISSCROSS ZONE 2

Ride Selection Criteria

Type	Interval
Purpose	Increase aerobic capacity, muscular endurance, and pedaling efficiency
Intensity	Aerobic
Zones	2
% Maximum HR	60%–70%
% Threshold HR	~70%–80%
Mesocycle	Preparation 1
Terrain	Flat, rolling
Time	1–2.5 hours
Heart Zones Points	~100–250 (maximum and threshold)

Set(s) by Rider's Fitness Level

	Level 1	*Level 2*	*Level 3*	*Level 4*	*Level 5*
Number of Repeats	2	3	4	5	>6
Work Interval	15 min.	15 min.	15 min.	15 min.	15 min.
% Maximum HR	70%	70%	70%	70%	70%
Recovery Interval % for Maximum HR	60%	60%	60%	60%	60%
% Threshold HR	~80%	~80%	~80%	~80%	~80%
Recovery Interval % for Threshold HR	~70%	~70%	~70%	~70%	~70%
Cadence during Work Interval	70–75 rpm	70–75 rpm	70–75 rpm	70–75 rpm	70–75 rpm

Heart Rate Profile and Rider's Notes

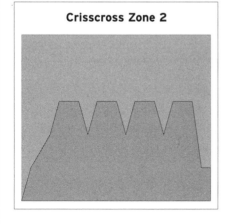

Crisscross Zone 2

1. Warm up 10–20 minutes to the bottom of Zone 2.
2. Slowly increase heart rate to 70% of maximum heart rate or ~80% of threshold heart rate, and sustain for 15 minutes at 70–75 rpm.
3. Recover heart rate.
4. Repeat interval according to your fitness level.
5. Cool down 10–20 minutes in Zone 1.

Ride Overview

This ride takes you on a tour through two zones, leaving you feeling energized and smiling. The goal is *not* to go into Zone 3, even on the hills. Pick a riding route through relatively flat to moderately rolling terrain. The idea is to spin your way up the hills using easy gearing and staying in the saddle. Select gears that keep your cadence between 70 and 75 rpm. This is a great opportunity to work on your pedal stroke and body position. Relax, enjoy the scenery, and spin your way along. You may choose not to use the large chainring. If that is the case, your cadence may be slightly higher than 90 rpm. Warm up for 10–20 minutes, gradually working your way up to the bottom of Zone 2. Slowly increase your heart rate to the top of Zone 2, and hold it there for 15 minutes; then recover to the bottom of Zone 2. Once you recover, repeat the interval according to your fitness level. Finish by cooling down for 10–20 minutes in Zone 1.

CRISSCROSS ZONE 3

Ride Selection Criteria

Type	Interval
Purpose	Increase aerobic capacity, muscular endurance, and pedaling efficiency
Intensity	Aerobic
Zones	3
% Maximum HR	70%–80%
% Threshold HR	~80%–90%
Mesocycle	Preparation 1
Terrain	Flat, rolling
Time	1–3 hours
Heart Zones Points	~195–275 (maximum and threshold)

Set(s) by Rider's Fitness Level

	Level 1	Level 2	Level 3	Level 4	Level 5
Number of Repeats	2	3	4	5	>6
Work Interval	15 min.	15 min.	15 min.	15 min.	15 min.
Work Interval % Maximum HR	80%	80%	80%	80%	80%
Recovery Interval % Maximum HR	70%	70%	70%	70%	70%
Work Interval % Threshold HR	~90%	~90%	~90%	~90%	~90%
Recovery Interval % Threshold HR	~80%	~80%	~80%	~80%	~80%
Cadence	70–75 rpm	70–75 rpm	70–75 rpm	70–75 rpm	70–75 rpm

Heart Rate Profile and Rider's Notes

Crisscross Zone 3

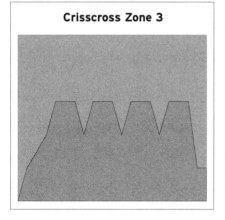

(Example for Level 3 rider)
1. Warm up 10–20 minutes to the bottom of Zone 3.
2. Slowly increase heart rate to 80% of maximum heart rate or ~90% of threshold heart rate, and sustain for 15 minutes at 70–75 rpm.
3. Recover.
4. Repeat interval according to your fitness level.
5. Cool down 10–20 minutes in Zone 2.

Note: For Preparation training, keep all heart rate intensities under 75 percent of maximum heart rate or ~85 percent of threshold heart rate.

Ride Overview

This ride takes you on a tour through three zones, leaving you feeling energized and smiling. The goal is *not* to go into Zone 4, even on the hills. Pick a riding route through relatively flat to moderately rolling terrain. Keep your cadence between 70 and 75 rpm, and stay seated. Relax, enjoy the scenery, and spin your way along. You may choose not to use the large chainring. If that is the case, your cadence may be slightly higher. Warm up for 10–20 minutes, gradually working your way up to the bottom of Zone 3. Slowly increase your heart rate to the top of Zone 3, and hold it there for 15 minutes; then recover to the bottom of Zone 3. Once you reach the bottom of Zone 3, repeat the interval according to your fitness level. Finish by cooling down for 10–20 minutes in Zone 2.

CRISSCROSS ZONE 4 (maximum heart rate only)

Ride Selection Criteria

Type	Interval
Purpose	Increase aerobic capacity, muscular strength and endurance, and lactic acid tolerance
Intensity	Threshold, nonaerobic
Zones	4
% Maximum HR	80%–90%
Mesocycle	Preparation 2, Competition
Terrain	Rolling
Time	1–3 hours
Heart Zones Points	~195–400 (maximum)

Set(s) by Rider's Fitness Level

	Level 1	*Level 2*	*Level 3*	*Level 4*	*Level 5*
Number of Repeats	—	1	2	3	4
% Maximum HR	—	80%–85%	80%–90%	80%–90%	80%–90%
Steady State	—	0 min.	30 sec.	30 sec.	45 sec.
Recovery Interval % Max HR	—	80%	80%	80%	80%
Cadence	—	80–95 rpm	80–95 rpm	80–95 rpm	80–95 rpm

Note: Level 2 riders may choose a lower intensity and not to hold a steady-state heart rate before recovery.

Heart Rate Profile and Rider's Notes

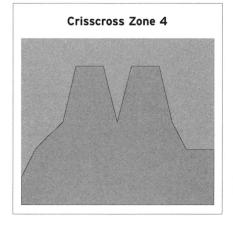

Crisscross Zone 4

1. Warm up gradually for 30 minutes to the bottom of Zone 4.
2. Gradually increase heart rate to 90% of maximum heart rate or ~100% of threshold heart rate, and sustain depending on fitness level. Hold a cadence of 80–95 rpm.
3. Recover to the bottom of Zone 4.
4. Repeat according to your fitness level.
5. Cool down 20 minutes in Zone 2.

Note: Not recommended for Level 1 or lower intensity Level 2 riders.

Ride Overview

This ride takes you on a tour through four zones. The goal is to sustain a high heart rate, working on improving your muscular endurance and lactate tolerance. Pick a riding route that is moderately rolling terrain. The idea is to crisscross your way from the bottom of Zone 4 to the top of Zone 4. Maintain your cadence of 80–95 rpm even on the hills by shifting gears. Stay focused once you reach the top of Zone 4, and hold a brief steady state heart rate.

Warm up for 30 minutes, gradually working your way up to the bottom of Zone 4. Slowly increase your heart rate to the top of Zone 4, and hold it in a steady state depending on your fitness level; then recover to the bottom of Zone 4. Once you reach the bottom of Zone 4, repeat the interval again according to your fitness level. Finish by cooling down for 20 minutes in Zone 2.

CRUISIN'

Ride Selection Criteria

Type	Interval
Purpose	Improve muscular strength and endurance; expand aerobic capacity
Intensity	Threshold
Zones	2–4
% Maximum HR	60%–85%
% Threshold HR	~70%–95%
Mesocycle	Preparation 2, Competition
Terrain	Flat
Time	50–90 minutes
Heart Zones Points	~100–200 (maximum and threshold)

Set(s) by Rider's Fitness Level

	Level 1	Level 2	Level 3	Level 4	Level 5
Number of Repeats	2	2	2	2	2
% Maximum HR	60%–70%	60%–80%	60%–85%	60%–85%	60%–85%
% Threshold HR	~70%–80%	~70%–90%	~70%–95%	~70%–95%	~70%–95%
Work Interval	3 min.	5 min.	8 min.	10 min.	12 min.
Recovery Interval % Maximum HR	60%	60%	60%	60%	60%
Recovery Interval % Threshold HR	~70%	~70%	~70%	~70%	~70%

Heart Rate Profile and Rider's Notes

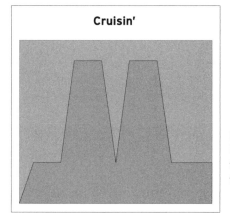

Cruisin'

1. Warm up 20 minutes to Zone 2.
2. Increase heart rate for 3–12 minutes depending on fitness level.
3. Recover to the bottom of Zone 2.
4. Repeat interval.
5. Cool down 20–30 minutes in Zone 2.

Notes: Increase number of repeats as you get fitter; increase heart rate intensity as you get fitter, but not to exceed 85% of maximum heart rate or ~95% of threshold heart rate.

Ride Overview

Pick a relatively flat course, and warm up for a minimum of 20 minutes. This ride consists of two repeats in a 3–12-minute interval, depending on your fitness level and cycling goals. The purpose of the ride is to improve your ability to ride in a relatively big gear at a relatively high cadence for an extended period of time. For fitness Levels 1 and 2 riders, the intensity builds from the bottom of Zone 2 to either the bottom of Zone 3 or the bottom of Zone 4. For fitness Levels 3–5 riders, the intensity builds from the bottom of Zone 2 to the midpoint of Zone 4. Recovery for all levels is at the bottom of Zone 2. Once you have recovered, immediately begin the next interval. Repeat this interval. Cool down 20–30 minutes in Zone 2.

EASY RIDER 1

Ride Selection Criteria

Type	Recovery
Purpose	Active recovery and technique
Intensity	Aerobic
Zones	1–2
% Maximum HR	Less than 65%
% Threshold HR	Less than ~75%
Mesocycle	Preparation 1, Preparation 2, Competition, Transition
Terrain	Flat, rolling
Time	30 minutes–2 hours
Heart Zones Points	~60–240 (maximum and threshold)

Set(s) by Rider's Fitness Level

	Level 1	*Level 2*	*Level 3*	*Level 4*	*Level 5*
% Maximum HR	<65%	<65%	<65%	<65%	<65%
% Threshold HR	<75%	<75%	<75%	<75%	<75%
Cadence	80–95 rpm	80–95 rpm	80–95 rpm	80–95 rpm	80–95 rpm

Heart Rate Profile and Rider's Notes

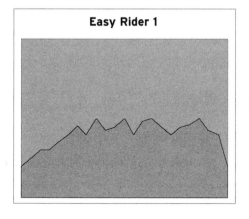

Easy Rider 1

1. Pick a flat to rolling terrain and easy gearing.
2. Stay under 65% of maximum heart rate or ~75% of threshold heart rate, working on body position, pedal stroke, and cadence.

Ride Overview

This is easy riding designed to give your body a chance to recover but still stay in the saddle and work on some technique. The goal is to stay under 65 percent of maximum heart rate or ~75 percent of threshold heart rate. Pick a ride that is relatively flat. If you have hills, use an easy gear and small chainring to spin your way to the top while staying seated. This is a "feel good" ride that allows you to smell the roses or chat with your training partner. Work on your body position, pedal stroke, and cadence. Your legs should feel relaxed as noodles. Ride easy, relaxing every muscle in your body and letting your mind go. Do whatever you need to do to keep your heart rate low—easier said than done.

EASY RIDER 2

Ride Selection Criteria

Type	Combination/recovery
Purpose	Active recovery and technique
Intensity	Aerobic
Zones	1–3
% Maximum HR	Less than 75%
% Threshold HR	Less than ~85%
Mesocycle	Preparation 1, Preparation 2, Transition
Terrain	Flat, rolling
Time	30 minutes–2 hours
Heart Zones Points	~60–240 (maximum and threshold)

Set(s) by Rider's Fitness Level

	Level 1	*Level 2*	*Level 3*	*Level 4*	*Level 5*
% Maximum HR	<75%	<75%	<75%	<75%	<75%
% Threshold HR	<85%	<85%	<85%	<85%	<85%
Cadence	80–95 rpm	80–95 rpm	80–95 rpm	80–95 rpm	80–95 rpm
Spin-Ups	3	4	5	6	7

Heart Rate Profile and Rider's Notes

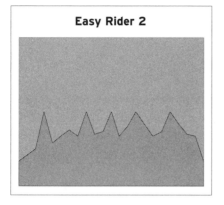

Easy Rider 2

1. Pick a flat to rolling terrain and easy gearing.
2. Stay under 75% of maximum heart rate or 85% of threshold heart rate, working on body position, pedal stroke, and cadence.
3. Intersperse Spin-Ups according to fitness level throughout the ride. (Spin-Ups: In easy to moderate gearing, start from 60 rpm and build 10 rpm every 10 seconds for 1 minute.)

Ride Overview

This is easy riding designed to give your body a chance to recover but still stay in the saddle and work on some technique. The goal is to stay under 75 percent of maximum heart rate or 85 percent of threshold heart rate. Pick a ride that is relatively flat. If you have hills, use an easy gear and small chainring to spin your way to the top while staying seated. Intersperse Spin-Ups for form and speed work throughout the ride according to your fitness level.

EASY RIDER 3

Ride Selection Criteria

Type	Combination/recovery
Purpose	Active recovery and technique
Intensity	Aerobic
Zones	1–3
% Maximum HR	65%–80%
% Threshold HR	~75%–90%
Mesocycle	Preparation 1, Preparation 2
Terrain	Flat, rolling
Time	50 minutes–2 hours
Heart Zones Points	~120–280 (maximum and threshold)

Set(s) by Rider's Fitness Level

	Level 1	*Level 2*	*Level 3*	*Level 4*	*Level 5*
% Maximum HR	65%–80%	65%–80%	65%–80%	65%–80%	65%–80%
% Threshold HR	~75%–90%	~75%–90%	~75%–90%	~75%–90%	~75%–90%
Cadence	80–95 rpm	80–95 rpm	80–95 rpm	80–95 rpm	80–95 rpm
Sprints	10 sec.	10 sec.	15 sec.	15 sec.	15 sec.
Number of Sprints	3	6	9	12	15

Heart Rate Profile and Rider's Notes

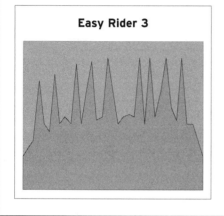

Easy Rider 3

1. Pick flat to rolling terrain and easy gearing.
2. Stay under 80% of maximum heart rate or ~90% of threshold heart rate (except when performing sprints), working on body position, pedal stroke, and cadence.
3. Intersperse sprints according to fitness level throughout the ride.

Ride Overview

This is easy riding designed to give your body a chance to recover but still stay in the saddle and work on some technique. The goal is to stay under 80 percent of maximum heart rate or roughly 90 percent of threshold heart rate. Pick a ride that is relatively flat. If you have hills, use an easy gear and small chainring to spin your way to the top while staying seated. Intersperse sprints for speed work throughout the ride according to your fitness level. Work on your body position, pedal stroke, and cadence. Give an all-out effort on your sprints and quickly return to an easy pace.

FIX IT

Ride Selection Criteria

Type	Combination
Purpose	Building aerobic capacity and endurance, muscular strength, and leg speed
Intensity	Aerobic
Zones	2–3
% Maximum HR	60%–80%
% Threshold HR	~70%–90%
Mesocycle	Preparation 1 and 2, Competition
Terrain	Flat, rolling
Time	1–2 hours
Heart Zones Points	~150–300 (maximum and threshold)

Set(s) by Rider's Fitness Level

	Level 1	Level 2	Level 3	Level 4	Level 5
% Maximum HR	60%–70%	60%–80%	60%–80%	60%–80%	60%–80%
% Threshold HR	~70%–80%	~70%–90%	~70%–90%	~70%–90%	~70%–90%

Rider's Notes

1. Warm up for 20 minutes.
2. Set gearing for strength level.
3. Ride flat to rolling course in Zones 2 and 3 without changing gearing.
4. Cool down 20 minutes.

Note: For Preparation 1 training, keep all heart rate intensities under 75% of maximum heart rate or 85% of threshold heart rate.

Ride Overview

This ride is best done initially on flat terrain; then as you get stronger, gradually add hills. Give yourself a good 20-minute warm-up before setting your gearing for the rest of the ride. When you set your gearing, choose what is appropriate for your strength level. Use a small chainring (39–42) and a large to medium cog (15–19). This ride will build endurance, strength, and leg speed.

GALACTIC

Ride Selection Criteria

Type	Steady state
Purpose	Establish high power output; improve tolerance and buffering of lactic acid
Intensity	Threshold
Zones	2–5 (maximum); 2–5a (threshold)
% Maximum HR	60%–90%
% Threshold HR	~70%–105+%
Mesocycle	Preparation 2, Competition
Terrain	Flat, rolling
Time	1–2 hours
Heart Zones Points	~140–400 (maximum); ~140–480 (threshold)

Set(s) by Rider's Fitness Level

	Level 1	Level 2	Level 3	Level 4	Level 5
Number of Repeats	1	2	3	4	4
% Maximum HR	80%	85%	90%	90%	90%
% Threshold HR	~100%	~100%	~105+%	~105+%	~105+%
Threshold Work Interval	2 min.	3 min.	6 min.	10 min.	14 min.
Threshold Recovery Interval	1 min.	1 min.	2 min.	2:30 min.	3:30 min.
Work-Recovery Ratio	2:1	3:1	3:1	4:1	4:1
Cadence	90–100 rpm	90–100 rpm	90–100 rpm	90–100 rpm	90–100 rpm

Heart Rate Profile and Rider's Notes

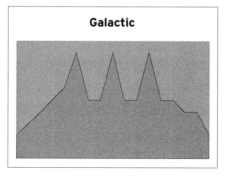

Galactic

(Example for Level 3 rider)
1. Warm up for 20–30 minutes.
2. Do three 6-minute threshold Intervals with 2 minutes of rest (high cadence with little or no resistance on recovery) between repeats.
3. Cool down 20–30 minutes.

Ride Overview

Training at this intensity is to be done only after developing a solid aerobic base during the base and endurance phases or Block 1 of training. This training is best described as "hard": Your breathing will be labored, and your muscles will fatigue. The payoff for these hard training sessions will be the ability to sustain a higher power output or speed for a longer period of time. Choose flat to rolling terrain.

Warm up for 20–30 minutes, and begin intervals according to your fitness level. You will be at or slightly above your threshold heart rate. Cadence will be between 90 and 100 rpm. This will be an "uncomfortable pace" as you push your threshold higher, enabling you to ride faster for longer. Keep your cadence high on your rest intervals (80–100 rpm). Finish your ride with a 20–30-minute cool-down.

HEAD FOR THE HILLS

Ride Selection Criteria

Type	Interval
Purpose	Increase aerobic capacity, improve pedaling efficiency, and increase power output
Intensity	Nonaerobic
Zones	3–4
% Maximum HR	75%–90%
% Threshold HR	~85%–100+%
Mesocycle	Preparation 2, Competition
Terrain	Hills
Time	1–1.5 hours
Heart Zones Points	~70–265 (maximum and threshold)

Set(s) by Rider's Fitness Level

	Level 1	Level 2	Level 3	Level 4	Level 5
Number of repeats	1–2	3–5	6–8	up to 9	>10
% Maximum HR	70%–75%	75%–80%	75%–90%	75%–90%	75%–90%
% Threshold HR	~80%–85%	~85%–90%	~85%–100+%	~85%–100+%	~85%–100+%
Work Interval (min)	1:30 min.	1:30 min.	1:30 min.	1:30 min.	1:30 min.
Recovery Interval % Maximum HR	70%	70%	70%	70%	70%
Recovery Interval % Threshold HR	~80%	~80%	~80%	~80%	~80%

Heart Rate Profile and Rider's Notes

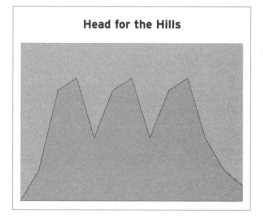

Head for the Hills

(Example for Level 3 rider)
1. Warm up for 30 minutes.
2. Increase heart rate to 75% of maximum or ~85% of threshold for 30 seconds at 70 rpm; then accelerate cadence to 95 rpm for 1 minute.
3. Recover heart rate.
4. Repeat interval according to your fitness level.
5. Cool down 20–30 minutes in Zone 2.

Ride Overview

To manage hilly terrain successfully, you must minimize your fatigue while climbing and become more efficient in your pedaling stroke. You will want to warm up at least 30 minutes at an easy pace before doing this series of cadence surges. Find a nice long, gradual hill or a series of gradual hills. Pick a gear in which you can ride at 70 rpm and 75 percent of your maximum heart rate or ~85 percent of your threshold heart rate for 30 seconds; then accelerate hard, stay seated, and increase your cadence to 95 rpm for 1 minute as you continue to climb. Slow your cadence back to 70 rpm, and repeat the interval once your heart rate has recovered to the bottom of Zone 3. You may continue these accelerations until you cannot maintain 95 rpm for 1 minute or repeat the interval according to your fitness level. Cool down with an easy pace for 20–30 minutes. Initially, you may be able to do only a few accelerations on the hills, but keep trying. They will get easier as you get fitter.

HICCUP

Ride Selection Criteria

Type	Interval
Purpose	Increase muscular strength and nonaerobic power output
Intensity	Nonaerobic
Zones	2–5 (maximum HR); 2–5b (threshold HR)
% Maximum HR	60%–90+%
% Threshold HR	~70%–110+%
Mesocycle	Preparation 2, Competition
Terrain	Hills
Time	1.5–2.5 hours
Heart Zones Points	175–300 (maximum); ~175–320 (threshold)

Set(s) by Rider's Fitness Level

	Level 1	*Level 2*	*Level 3*	*Level 4*	*Level 5*
Number of Repeats	—	2	3	4	5
% Maximum HR	—	60%–85%	60%–90%	60%–90+%	60%–90+%
% Threshold HR	—	~70%–95%	~70%–100+%	~70%–110+%	~70%–110+%
Work Interval	—	20 sec.	30 sec.	45 sec.	60 sec.
Recovery Interval	—	3:30 min.	5:00 min.	7:30 min.	10:00 min.
Work-Recovery Ratio	—	1:10	1:10	1:10	1:10

Heart Rate Profile and Rider's Notes

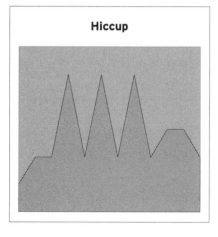

Hiccup

1. Warm up for 20 minutes.
2. Ride with a fast cadence halfway up the hill; then shift to the big chainring, stand, and sprint to the top of the hill.
3. Recover and repeat according to fitness level.
4. Cool down or continue to ride in Zone 3 with a cadence of 80–95 rpm.

Note: Not recommended for Level 1 riders.

Ride Overview

Hills are your friends; they make you stronger, and sooner or later they will be in your training plan.

Warm up for a minimum of 20 minutes, and then start your first hill sprint. Find a gradual hill (4 to 5 percent) that is approximately 200–400 yards long.

In an easy gear with a high cadence (95 rpm), spin halfway up the hill; then shift into your big chainring, stand, and sprint all-out to the top of the hill or according to your fitness level time.

Recover and then repeat according to your fitness level. As you get stronger, shift to harder gearing. Try to finish your last sprint strong, as if you were sprinting to the finish line.

Cool down 20–30 minutes, or continue a Zone 3 ride with 80–95 rpm cadence.

HOLY SMOKES

Ride Selection Criteria

Type	Interval
Purpose	Increase the rate of oxygen delivery to the muscles or VO_2 capacity
Intensity	Aerobic
Zones	2–5 (maximum HR); 2–5b (threshold)
% Maximum HR	60%–95%
% Threshold HR	100%–~110%
Mesocycle	Preparation 2, Competition
Terrain	Flat, rolling
Time	1–1.5 hours
Heart Zones Points	~125–225 (maximum); ~125–365 (threshold)

Set(s) by Rider's Fitness Level

	Level 1	Level 2	Level 3	Level 4	Level 5
Number of Sets	—	—	1–2	2	2
Rest between Sets	—	—	6 min.	8 min.	10 min.
Number of Repeats	—	—	3–4	3–4	3–4
Effort	—	—	As hard as possible	As hard as possible	As hard as possible
Work Interval	—	—	30 sec./45 sec.	1 min./2 min.	3 min./4 min.
Recovery Interval	—	—	20 sec./30 sec.	45 sec./90 sec.	2 sec./3 min.
Work-Recovery Ratio	—	—	3:2	4:3	3:2–4:3
Cadence on Work Interval	—	—	90–100 rpm	90–100 rpm	90–100 rpm

Heart Rate Profile and Rider's Notes

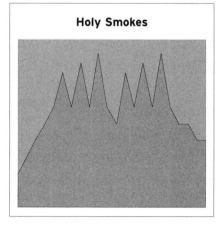

Holy Smokes

(Example for Level 3 rider)
1. Warm up for 20 minutes.
2. First set: Three 30-second VO_2 intervals with 20 seconds of rest.
3. Take 6 minutes for recovery between sets at an easy pedal.
4. Second set: Three 45-second VO_2 intervals with 30 seconds of rest.
5. Cool down 20 minutes.

Ride Overview

This ride is not recommended for Level 1 or Level 2 riders.

VO_2 intervals are meant to boost your oxygen consumption levels. A high VO_2max is a good indication of fitness and an essential component of well-trained endurance athletes. These intervals should be done only after you've established a strong aerobic base in Block 1 training. You will ride as hard as you can for the work interval. You will monitor your intensity by how you feel rather than heart rate on the short intervals, and you will use your heart rate monitor during the longer intervals.

Choose flat to rolling terrain, and start with a 20–30-minute warm-up. Repeat sets and repeats according to fitness level, cadence between 90 and 100 rpm. During the rest intervals, keep a high cadence (80–100) with easy gearing.

Cool down 20–30 minutes.

JUMPIN' JIMINIE

Ride Selection Criteria

Type	Combination
Purpose	Improve explosive power
Intensity	Aerobic, ATP-PC
Zones	2–4
% Maximum HR	60%–80+%
% Threshold HR	~70%–90+%
Mesocycle	Preparation 2, Competition
Terrain	Flat, rolling
Time	1.5–2.5 hours
Heart Zones Points	~250–375 (maximum and threshold)

Set(s) by Rider's Fitness Level

	Level 1	*Level 2*	*Level 3*	*Level 4*	*Level 5*
Sets	—	2	3	4	5
Repeats	—	5	5	5	5
Rest between Sets	—	5 min.	5 min.	5 min.	5 min.
% Maximum HR	—	60%–80%	60%–80+%	60%–80+%	60%–80+%
% Threshold HR	—	~70%–90%	~70%–90+%	~70%–90+%	~70%–90+%
Jumps	—	8–10 sec.	8–10 sec.	8–10 sec.	8–10 sec.
Recovery	—	1 min.	1 min.	1 min.	1 min.
Work-to-Recovery Ratio	—	1:7	1:7	1:7	1:7

Heart Rate Profile and Rider's Notes

Jumpin' Jiminie

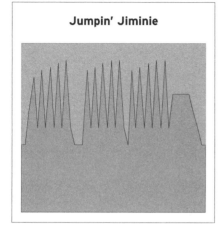

(Example for Level 3 shown)
1. Warm up for 30 minutes in Zones 2 and 3.
2. Do three sets of five 8–10-second Jumps with a 1-minute recovery in between Jumps and a 5-minute recovery between sets.
3. Do a 30-minute tempo ride in Zone 3 at 70–75 rpm.
4. Cool down 20 minutes.

Notes: Not recommended for Level 1 riders. Jumps are short, high-speed bursts with resistance. They increase ATP-PC output using energy sources stored in the muscles.

Ride Overview

Choose flat to rolling terrain. Warm up for 30 minutes in Zones 2 and 3. Begin Jump sets according to your fitness level. Each Jump is between 8 and 10 seconds or 10–12 revolutions of the crank (each leg) at high cadence. You can best monitor your intensity by how you feel due to the lag, or response, time of your heart rate during these intervals. Recover for 1 minute between Jumps and 5 minutes between sets. Jumps are designed to increase your explosive power for warp-speed acceleration when you need it.

KOWABUNGA

Ride Selection Criteria

Type	Combination
Purpose	Building aerobic endurance, muscular strength
Intensity	Aerobic
Zones	2–4
% Maximum HR	65%–90%
% Threshold HR	~75%–100%
Mesocycle	Preparation 2, Competition
Terrain	Flat, rolling, and hills
Time	1.5–2.5 hours
Heart Zones Points	~170–400 (maximum and threshold)

Set(s) by Rider's Fitness Level

Steady State Set	Level 1	Level 2	Level 3	Level 4	Level 5
Number of Repeats	—	2	2	2–3	2–3
% Maximum HR	—	~80%	~85%	~90%	~90%
% Threshold HR	—	~100%	~100%	~100%	~100%
Work Interval	—	8 min.	15 min.	20 min.	20 min.
Recovery Interval	—	8 min.	5 min.	5 min.	5 min.
Work-Recovery Ratio	—	1:1	3:1	4:1	4:1
Cadence	—	85–95 rpm	85–95 rpm	85–95 rpm	85–95 rpm

Muscular Strength/ Tension Set	Level 1	Level 2	Level 3	Level 4	Level 5
Number of Repeats	1	2	3	3	3
% Maximum HR	—	~70%–75%	~70%–75%	~70%–75%	~70%–75%
% Threshold HR	—	~80%–85%	~80%–85%	~80%–85%	~80%–85%
Work Interval	—	5 min.	5 min.	5 min.	5 min.
Recovery Interval	—	10 min.	5 min.	5 min.	5 min.
Work-Recovery Ratio	—	1:2	1:1	1:1	1:1
Cadence	—	50 rpm	50 rpm	50 rpm	50 rpm

Heart Rate Profile and Rider's Notes

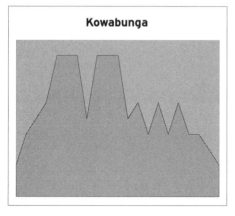

Kowabunga

1. Warm up for 15–20 minutes.
2. Repeat steady state intervals per fitness level at 3–5 bpm below threshold heart rate. Check fitness level for heart rate percentages. Cadence is 85–95 rpm.
3. Find a hill with 4%–5% grade. Repeat muscle strength intervals per fitness level; cadence is 50 rpm, large gears.
4. Cool down 15–20 minutes.

Notes: Not recommended for Level 1 riders. "~Threshold percentage" means to ride three to five beats below threshold heart rate. If you are using the maximum heart rate program and know your threshold heart rate, use that number minus three to five beats instead of suggested percentages.

Ride Description

This is a "black diamond" ride that will have you hollering "Kowabunga!" Warm up a minimum of 15–20 minutes in an easy gear. The steady state intervals will be done on flat to rolling terrain at a cadence of 85–90 rpm and a heart rate of 3–5 bpm below your threshold. These intervals are designed to build your aerobic endurance and muscular strength so you can ride farther and faster. Ride these intervals according to your fitness level, and as you get fitter, increase the work interval and decrease the rest interval. The muscle strength/tension set is strengthening your legs much like lifting weights in a gym. The intervals are done on a gradual hill, 4 to 5 percent, at a low cadence (50 rpm), low heart rate (comfortable to talk), and large gears. Increase the repeats or your work-recovery intervals as you get fitter. Keep a one-to-one ratio between your work intervals and recovery intervals. Be aware of your knees, and back off on the work interval and repeats if they begin to hurt. Cool down with a minimum of 15–20 minutes of easy pedaling.

PYRAMID SCHEME 1

Ride Selection Criteria

Type	Interval
Purpose	Increase aerobic capacity; improve VO_2 and lactic acid tolerance
Intensity	Aerobic
Zones	2–3
% Maximum HR	60%–75%
% Threshold HR	~70%–85%
Mesocycle	Preparation 1
Terrain	Flat, rolling
Time	60–100 minutes
Heart Zones Points	~130–150 (maximum and threshold)

Set(s) by Rider's Fitness Level

	Level 1	Level 2	Level 3	Level 4	Level 5
% Maximum HR	60%–75%	60%–75%	60%–75%	60%–75%	60%–75%
% Threshold HR	~70%–85%	~70%–85%	~70%–85%	~70%–85%	~70%–85%
Work-Recovery Ratio	1:1	1:1	1:1	1:1	1:1
Cadence	85–90 rpm	85–90 rpm	85–90 rpm	85–90 rpm	85–90 rpm

Heart Rate Profile and Rider's Notes

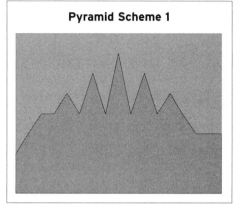

Pyramid Scheme 1

1. Warm up 15–30 minutes. Pick a flat to rolling course.
2. Ride 2 minutes at 65% maximum or ~75% threshold heart rate; then 2-minute recovery.
3. Ride 3 minutes at 70% maximum or ~80% threshold heart rate; then 3-minute recovery.
4. Ride 4 minutes at 75% maximum or ~85% threshold heart rate; then 4-minute recovery.
5. Ride 3 minutes at 70% maximum or ~80% threshold heart rate; then 3-minute recovery.
6. Ride 2 minutes at 65% maximum or ~75% threshold heart rate; then 2-minute recovery.
7. Cool down 15–30 minutes in Zone 2.

Note: Recovery is 60% of maximum heart rate or ~70% of threshold heart rate

Ride Overview

This ride gradually gets more challenging but still stays within your aerobic zones. The work intervals increase in time and intensity, and the recovery time is equal to the preceding work interval. Pick a flat to rolling course, and begin the pyramid ride after completely warming up (15–30 minutes).

The work intervals start at 2 minutes, go up to 3 minutes, then 4 minutes, and then back down to 3 and 2. They start from 65–75 percent of maximum heart rate or 75–85 percent of threshold heart rate.

As an option, you may choose to reach a certain heart rate percentage and then drop in intensity instead of continuing higher.

To make this ride more challenging, increase the minutes at each percentage, making sure you recover an equal amount of time as the work interval.

Cool down gradually in Zone 2 for 15–30 minutes.

PYRAMID SCHEME 2

Ride Selection Criteria

Type	Interval
Purpose	Increase aerobic capacity; improve VO_2 and lactic acid tolerance
Intensity	Aerobic, threshold, nonaerobic
Zones	2–5 (maximum); 2–5b (threshold)
% Maximum HR	60%–90%
% Threshold HR	~70%–110%
Mesocycle	Preparation 2, Competition
Terrain	Flat, rolling
Time	70–100 minutes
Heart Zones Points	~130–210 (maximum); ~130–220 (threshold)

Set(s) by Rider's Fitness Level

	Level 1	*Level 2*	*Level 3*	*Level 4*	*Level 5*
% Maximum HR	60%–75%	60%–80%	60%–85%	60%–90+%	60%–90+%
% Threshold HR	~70%–85%	~70%–90%	~70%–95%	~70%–110%	~70%–110%
Work-Recovery Ratio	1:1	1:1	1:1	1:1	1:1

Heart Rate Profile and Rider's Notes

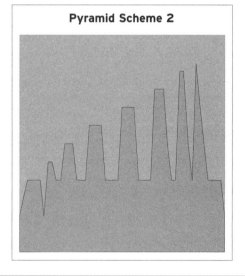

Pyramid Scheme 2

1. Warm up 15–30 minutes. Pick a flat to rolling course.
2. Ride 1 minute at 60% maximum or ~70% threshold heart rate; then 1-minute recovery.
3. Ride 2 minutes at 65% maximum or ~75% threshold heart rate; then 2-minute recovery.
4. Ride 3 minutes at 70% maximum or ~80% threshold heart rate; then 3-minute recovery.
5. Ride 4 minutes at 75% maximum or ~85% threshold heart rate; then 4-minute recovery.
6. Ride 3 minutes at 85% maximum or ~95% threshold heart rate; then 3-minute recovery.
7. Ride 2 minutes at 90% maximum or ~105% threshold heart rate; then 2-minute recovery.
8. Ride 1 minute at 90+% maximum or ~110% threshold heart rate; then 1-minute recovery.
9. Cool down 15–30 minutes in Zone 2.

Ride Overview

This ride gradually gets more challenging. The work intervals increase in time and intensity, and the recovery time is equal to the preceding work interval. Pick a flat to rolling course and begin the pyramid ride after completely warming up (15–30 minutes).

The work intervals in minutes are 1, 2, 3, 4, 3, 2, and 1. They build from 60 to over 90 percent of maximum heart rate or ~70 percent–110 percent of threshold heart rate.

As an option, you may choose to reach a certain heart rate percentage and then drop in intensity instead of continuing higher.

To make this ride more challenging, increase the minutes at each percentage, making sure you recover an equal amount of time as the work interval.

Cool down gradually in Zone 2 for 15–30 minutes.

ROCK STEADY

Ride Selection Criteria

Type	Steady state
Purpose	Build aerobic and muscular endurance
Intensity	Aerobic
Zones	2–4
% Maximum HR	60%–90%, depending on fitness level
% Threshold HR	3–5 bpm below threshold heart rate
Mesocycle	Preparation 1, Preparation 2
Terrain	Flat, rolling
Time	1–2.5 hours
Heart Zones Points	~80–440 (maximum and threshold)

Set(s) by Rider's Fitness Level

	Level 1	*Level 2*	*Level 3*	*Level 4*	*Level 5*
Number of Repeats	1	2	3	4	4
% Maximum HR	~75%	~80%	~85%	~85%	~90%
Heart Rate	<100%	<100%	<100%	<100%	<100%
Work Interval	10 min.	12 min.	14 min.	16 min.	20 min.
Recovery Interval	5 min.	4 min.	3:30 min.	4 min.	5 min.
Work-Recovery Ratio	2:1	3:1	4:1	4:1	4:1
Cadence	90–100 rpm	90–100 rpm	90–100 rpm	90–100 rpm	90–100 rpm

Heart Rate Profile and Rider's Notes

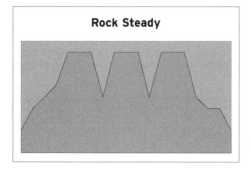

Rock Steady

1. Warm up for 15–20 minutes.
2. Repeat steady state intervals per fitness level at 3–5 bpm below threshold or according to your fitness level. Cadence is 90–100 rpm.
3. Cool down 15–20 minutes.

Note: We suggest you use your threshold heart rate number even if you are using maximum heart rate to anchor your heart zones.

Ride Overview

Rock Steady is designed to increase your aerobic capacity and endurance. This ride can be as challenging as you want to make it by raising the steady state interval time and/or increasing the intensity. The length of the ride may also be increased by adding riding time in Zones 2 and 3 prior to the steady state intervals or after. Cadence during the steady state intervals should be 90–100 rpm on flat to rolling terrain.

SIGN HERE, PRESS HARD

Ride Selection Criteria

Type	Interval
Purpose	To improve high-speed rhythm and coordination during all-out efforts
Intensity	Aerobic, nonaerobic, ATP-PC
Zones	"All-out"
% Maximum HR	~80+%–~90+%
% Threshold HR	~90+%–~110+%
Mesocycle	Preparation 2, Competition
Terrain	Flat, rolling
Time	1–3 hours
Heart Zones Points	100–300 (maximum); 100–320 (threshold)

Set(s) by Rider's Fitness Level

	Level 1	Level 2	Level 3	Level 4	Level 5
Number of Sets	—	1	2	2	2
Number of Repeats	—	2	2	3	3
% Maximum HR	—	~80+%	~85+%	~90+%	~90+%
% Threshold HR	—	~90+%	~95+%	~105+%	~110+%
Sprint	—	15 sec.	30 sec.	45 sec.	60 sec.
Cadence	—	135–160 rpm	135–160 rpm	135–160 rpm	135–160 rpm
Recovery between Repeats	—	5 min.	10 min.	17 min.	20 min.
Work-Recovery Ratio	—	1:20	1:20	1:20	1:20

Heart Rate Profile and Rider's Notes

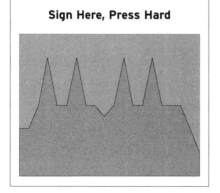

Sign Here, Press Hard

1. Warm up for 20 minutes.
2. On flat to rolling terrain, ride easy in Zone 3, cadence 80–95 rpm.
3. Intersperse sprints according to fitness level.
4. Cool down 20 minutes.

Ride Overview

Warm up 20 minutes in Zones 2 and 3 on flat to rolling terrain. Intersperse into your endurance ride, pick out a sign anywhere from 100 to 300 yards away, and challenge yourself or your riding partner to a sprint to the sign. Make sure the sign is not a stop sign! If you do not use yards, then sprint according to the time for your fitness level. You will see some high heart rate numbers, especially on the longer sprints. On the longer sprints your heart rate monitor will lag behind your effort. Give an all-out effort and don't be too concerned with your heart rate number. This is a great way to work on your fast starts and pedaling speed along with having some fun!

SILVER STREAK

Ride Selection Criteria

Type	Combination
Purpose	Overall training with variations in intensity and cadence
Intensity	Aerobic, threshold, nonaerobic, ATP-PC
Zones	2–5 (maximum); 2–5a (threshold)
% Maximum HR	60%–~90%
% Threshold HR	~70%–105+%
Mesocycle	Preparation 2, Competition
Terrain	Varied
Time	1–3 hours
Heart Zones Points	Varies

Set(s) by Rider's Fitness Level

	Level 1	Level 2	Level 3	Level 4	Level 5
% Maximum HR	—	60%–~85%	60%–~90%	60%–~90%	60%–~90+%
% Threshold HR	—	~70%–00%	~70%–100%	~70%–100+%	~70%–105+%

Rider's Notes

1. Warm up 15–20 minutes.
2. Focus on high intensity during all climbs according to fitness level. Stay in low intensity during descents.
3. On short hills (5–15 seconds), attack with 70–80 rpm and hard gearing.
4. On long hills (8–15 minutes), ride at 3–5 beats below threshold heart rate or Zone 4, and every minute accelerate the cadence to 95 rpm for 15 seconds.
5. On flats, ride at 80–95 rpm in Zone 3.
6. Ride two 8–15-second sprints, all-out effort, with 5 minutes of recovery in between.
7. Cool down 20–30 minutes in Zone 2.

Ride Overview

This is a ride where the terrain will present the various challenges. You will want to choose terrain that includes flats, rolling terrain, long hills, and short hills. Just remember that on the long hills or climbs (8–15 minutes), you are going to ride hard at just below threshold heart rate (or Zone 4) while using the descents as recovery time. Every minute on the climb, accelerate your cadence to 95 rpm for 15 seconds in the same gear. This will push your heart rate and your power output higher.

Attack the short hills or rollers (5–15 seconds) in a big gear at 70–80 rpm; then recover back down until you come to another short hill.

On the flats, ride at 80–95 rpm and keep your heart rate in Zone 3.

Finish your ride with two (8–15-second) all-out sprints, with a 5-minute recovery in between.

Cool down 20–30 minutes in Zone 2.

TURTLE ROCK

Ride Selection Criteria

Type	Steady state
Purpose	Increase aerobic workload efficiency
Intensity	Aerobic
Zones	2–3
% Maximum HR	Less than 80%
% Threshold HR	Less than 90%
Mesocycle	Preparation 1, Preparation 2, Competition
Terrain	Flat, tolling
Time	1.25–3 hours
Heart Zones Points	~200–540 (maximum and threshold)

Set(s) by Rider's Fitness Level

	Level 1	*Level 2*	*Level 3*	*Level 4*	*Level 5*
Number of Repeats	3	3	3	3	3 or more
% Maximum HR	70%–75%	75%–80%	75%–80%	75%–80%	75%–80%
% Threshold HR	~80%–85%	~85%–90%	~85%–90%	~85%–90%	~85%–90%
Work Interval	10 min.	14 min.	20 min.	30 min.	30 min.
Recovery Interval	5 min.	7 min.	10 min.	15 min.	15 min.
Work-Recovery Ratio	2:1	2:1	2:1	2:1	2:1
Cadence	70–75 rpm	70–75 rpm	70–75 rpm	70–75 rpm	70–75 rpm

Heart Rate Profile and Rider's Notes

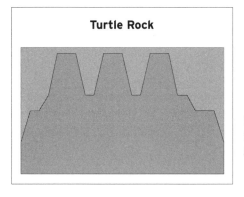

Turtle Rock

1. Warm up for 15–20 minutes.
2. Repeat steady state intervals according to fitness level; cadence at 70–75 rpm, moderately big gear.
3. Cool down 15–20 minutes.

Note: For Preparation 1 training, keep all heart rate intensities below 75% of maximum heart rate or 85% of threshold heart rate.

Ride Overview

This ride is named after a mountain in the California Alps near the town of Markleeville. It is near the start and finish of the famed Death Ride. Both the Death Ride and this ride are tests of your ability to stay steady, focused, and tenacious like a tortoise. Choose this ride in Block 1 of your training, and adjust the intervals for your fitness level. The goal is to spend time in the saddle building your aerobic base. The tempo or cadence is steady along with heart rate, which will be between 75 and 80 percent of your maximum or between ~85 and 90 percent of threshold. If you are in Preparation 1, keep heart rate intensities below 75 percent of maximum or 85 percent of threshold. Choose flat to rolling terrain and ride in a moderately big gear at 70–75 rpm. Warm up for 15–20 minutes, then choose the steady state work interval that best fits your fitness and training level. Finish with a 15–20-minute cool-down.

ASSESSMENT RIDES

AEROBIC TIME TRIAL

Ride Selection Criteria

Type	Assessment and steady state
Purpose	Measure fitness improvement
Intensity	Aerobic
Zones	2–3
% Maximum HR	75%
% Threshold HR	~85%
Mesocycle	Preparation 1, Preparation 2, Competition
Terrain	Flat, rolling
Time	45–60 minutes
Heart Zones Points	~90–180 (maximum and threshold)

Set(s) by Rider's Fitness Level

	Level 1	Level 2	Level 3	Level 4	Level 5
% Maximum HR	75%	75%	75%	75%	75%
% Threshold HR	~85%	~85%	~85%	~85%	~85%

Rider's Notes
1. Warm up 15–20 minutes.
2. Ride 5 miles at 75% of maximum heart rate or ~85% of threshold heart rate.
3. Stay in the same gear for the entire time.
4. Record your time.
5. Retest in a month.

Ride Overview

Choose a flat 5-mile section of road that has no stop signs, roaming dogs, or other distractions. After a 15–20-minute warm-up, ride 5 miles at 75 percent of your maximum heart rate or ~85 percent of your threshold heart rate. Stay in the same gear for the entire time trial. Record your time at the end. The conditions must be the same from one time trial test to the next. This includes the amount of rest since your last high-intensity ride, the length and intensity of your warm-up, the weather and road conditions, and the gear you used in the previous test. As you become fitter, your time will decrease. This is a good test to do once a month, especially as you increase your training intensity and training load.

ALL-OUT TRIP

Ride Selection Criteria

Type	Assessment
Purpose	Field test for maximum heart rate
Intensity	Nonaerobic
Zones	All
% Maximum HR	~90+%
Mesocycle	Preparation 1, Preparation 2, Competition
Terrain	Flat
Time	Less than 60 minutes
Heart Zones Points	~100–300

Set(s) by Rider's Fitness Level

	Level 1	*Level 2*	*Level 3*	*Level 4*	*Level 5*
Number of Repeats	—	2	2	2	2
Recovery Time	—	10 min.	10 min.	10 min.	10 min.

Heart Rate Profile and Rider's Notes

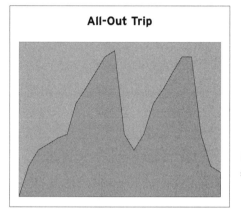

All-Out Trip

1. Warm up 20 minutes, easy spin in Zone 2.
2. Sprint 0.5 miles at full speed and all-out effort.
3. Slow down and recover 10 minutes with an easy pedal.
4. Repeat a second time.
5. Cool down 20–30 minutes.

Notes: Not recommended for Level 1 riders. Make sure you are fully rested before doing this test.

Ride Overview

This test takes you to a point near your maximum heart rate. Make sure you are fully rested before doing this test. Find a 1,000-meter or half-mile measured distance that is flat and has no obstructions. Warm up adequately 20–30 minutes. Sprint the distance as hard as you can, going full speed with a friend riding nearby to encourage you. Motivation is an essential factor in trying to get close to your true maximum heart rate. Do this twice. Recover for 10 minutes with easy pedaling. The second time should be more difficult than the first and probably will be the lower of the two numbers. Use the higher of the two numbers as your maximum heart rate for cycling.

CYCLING ECONOMY TEST

Ride Selection Criteria

Type	Assessment
Purpose	Measure climbing economy (efficiency)
Intensity	Aerobic
Zones	Choice
% HR	Choice
Mesocycle	Preparation 1, Preparation 2, Competition
Terrain	Hills
Time	More than 60 minutes
Heart Zones Points	~70–120 (maximum and threshold)

Heart Rate Profile and Rider's Notes

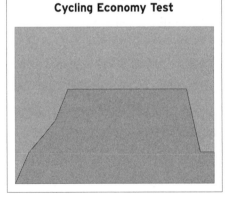

Cycling Economy Test

1. Warm up 20 minutes, easy spin in Zone 2.
2. Find a 1-mile hill. Start your chronograph or stopwatch. Climb at a steady heart rate and cadence.
3. Record time, heart rate, and cadence.
4. Repeat, trying different techniques, and record the data.
5. Cool down 20 minutes in Zone 2.

Ride Overview

Improving your cycling efficiency or your body's economy of motion is key to increasing your performance. Your power dictates how fast you can go for a period of time, but your economy or efficiency is how many miles to the gallon you get, which is critically important on longer rides. One way to test your efficiency is to find a hill about 1 mile long. Mark the beginning and the end of the hill. You are going to time how long it takes you to ride from the beginning to the end at a set heart rate and a set cadence. Ride the section again using different techniques such as different gearing, riding out of the saddle, and a different cadence. Through this process the goal is to determine the most efficient technique for climbing (the fastest method for the same energy expenditure).

HILL SPRINTS

Ride Selection Criteria

Type	Maximum heart rate assessment
Purpose	Field test for maximum heart rate
Intensity	Nonaerobic
Zones	All
% HR	Largest number you see on your HR monitor
Mesocycle	Preparation 1
Terrain	Hills
Time	45–90 minutes
Heart Zones Points	~100–130

Set(s) by Rider's Fitness Level

	Level 1	Level 2	Level 3	Level 4	Level 5
Number of Repeats	—	2	3	3	3
Recovery as % Maximum HR	—	70%	70%	70%	70%
Recovery Time	—	<5 min.	<5 min.	<5 min.	<5 min.

Heart Rate Profile and Rider's Notes

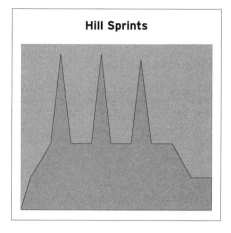

Hill Sprints

1. Warm up 20 minutes, easy spin in Zone 2.
2. Ride two to three all-out 1-minute sprints to the top of the hill according to your fitness level.
3. Recover to 70% of maximum heart rate or <5 minutes between sprints.
4. Cool down 20–30 minutes in Zone 2.

Note: Not recommended for Level 1 riders. Level 2 riders may want to perform a submax test to estimate maximum heart rate.

Ride Overview

Select a hill that you can sprint to the top of in approximately 1 minute. Do two to three all-out sprints to the top with very little rest in between. Use the "highest" number you see on your heart rate monitor as your estimated maximum heart rate.

LARGER THAN LIFE

Ride Selection Criteria

Type	Assessment
Purpose	Field test assessment for maximum heart rate
Intensity	Varies
Zones	The largest number you see on your heart rate monitor
Mesocycle	Preparation 1
Terrain	Flat
Time	Less than 60 minutes
Heart Zones Points	~100–125

Heart Rate Profile and Rider's Notes

Larger Than Life

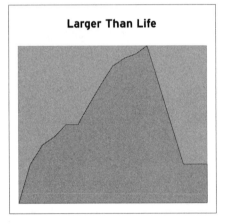

1. Warm up 20 minutes, easy spin to bottom of Zone 2 or a heart rate of 110 bpm.
2. Start chronograph or stopwatch, and every 15 seconds, increase your heart rate 5 bpm until your heart rate no longer rises.
3. Slow down and recover to 60% of maximum heart rate.
4. Cool down 20–30 minutes.

Note: Not recommended for Level 1 riders. Level 2 riders may want to perform a submax test to estimate maximum heart rate.

Ride Overview

This is a quick assessment that takes you near your maximum heart rate. Pick a flat stretch of road that is free of stops signs and vehicular traffic. Turn on your bike computer and heart rate monitor and warm up completely, 20–30 minutes. From the bottom of Zone 2 or 110 bpm, start your chronograph or stopwatch. Every 15 seconds, increase your heart rate 5 bpm until your heart rate no longer rises. When you reach a point of near exhaustion, slow down and recover. If your heart rate monitor does not store "peak" heart rate, mentally record the highest number you see. If you have given your best all-out effort, you are within 5–10 beats of maximum heart rate. When doing this test, make sure you are fully rested and mentally prepared to go all-out. Always have a friend with you for both safety and motivation.

RECOVERY INTERVAL RIDE

Ride Selection Criteria

Type	Assessment
Purpose	Fitness improvement test/increase in muscular endurance and aerobic capacity
Intensity	Aerobic, threshold, nonaerobic
Zones	2–5 (maximum); 2–5b (threshold)
% Maximum HR	50%–90+%
% Threshold HR	~60%–110%
Mesocycle	Preparation 1, Preparation 2, Competition
Terrain	Flat, rolling
Time	50 minutes–1.75 hours
Heart Zones Points	~120–230 (maximum and threshold)

Set(s) by Rider's Fitness Level

	Level 1	Level 2	Level 3	Level 4	Level 5
Number of Repeats	2	2	3	3	3
% Maximum HR	60%–75%	60%–80%	60%–85%	60%–90%	60%–90+%
% Threshold HR	~70%–85%	~70%–90%	~70%–95%	~70%–105%	~70%–110%
Work-Recovery Ratio	1:1	1:1	1:1	1:1	1:1
Cadence	80–95 rpm	80–95 rpm	80–95 rpm	80–95 rpm	80–95 rpm

Heart Rate Profile and **Rider's** Notes

Recovery Interval Ride

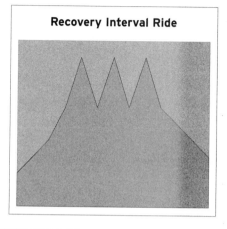

1. Warm up 15–20 minutes or until you are ready to ride hard.
2. Ride hard at 80–95 rpm according to your fitness level for 5 minutes; then drop down 5 mph for 5 minutes.
3. Repeat this hard effort and recovery interval two more times.
4. Record average heart rate, elapsed time, and average speed for the intervals.
5. Continue to ride or cool down for 15–20 minutes.

Ride Overview

Recovery heart rate or how **quickly** you recover from an exercise bout or work interval is a measurement **of how** fit you are. The faster your heart rate recovers, the fitter your cardiovascular system. This is an assessment you will periodically want to do to see **if your** training is working *for* you or working *against* you (overtraining).

This ride is a series of three **hard intervals** with three recoveries. Choose flat to rolling terrain. Warm up for **15–20** minutes or until you feel like you can ride hard. Ride hard for 5 minutes **at a fixed** speed and a cadence between 80 and 95 rpm. Level 1 riders should ride **under** 15 mph. Level 2 riders should ride under 18 mph; Level 3 riders, under **20 mph**; and Levels 4 and 5, 20+ mph.

After 5 minutes of hard ri**ding, drop** 5 miles per hour for the next 5 minutes. Repeat this hard effort **and recovery** interval two more times.

Record in your logbook **the following** information from the main set of your ride:

- Average heart rate
- Elapsed time
- Average speed

These numbers become **benchmark** numbers and allow you to measure your improvement and indivi**dualize your** training.

STEADY STATE RIDE

Ride Selection Criteria

Type	Assessment
Purpose	Assess fitness improvement
Intensity	Aerobic
Zones	Rider's choice
% HR	Choice
Mesocycle	Preparation 1, Preparation 2, **Competition**
Terrain	Flat, rolling
Time	30–90 minutes
Heart Zones Points	~90–180

Set(s) by Rider's Fitness Level

	Level 1	Level 2	Level 3	Level 4	Level 5
Distance	5 miles	10 miles	15 miles	20 miles	25 miles
Heart Rate	Avg.	Avg.	Avg.	Avg.	Avg.

Rider's Notes

1. Warm up 15–20 minutes.
2. Ride the course at a comfortable and constant speed.
3. Record average heart rate.
4. Retest once a month.

Ride Overview

Warm up for 15–20 minutes at a comfortable heart rate. For this steady state ride, you will be keeping a constant speed and taking your average heart rate at the end of the ride. You will want to hold a speed that is comfortable and choose a distance according to your riding fitness level. Choose a flat to rolling course or one that you know you can keep a constant speed. The key is not the distance you cover but the steady speed you hold. Try to hold a constant speed throughout the ride, and at the end you only have one key number to record—average heart rate.

Do this ride once a month to see if your average heart rate is dropping. Make sure you do this ride under the same conditions each time and the same speed in order to more accurately measure your improvement.

THRESHOLD CYCLING ROAD TEST

Ride Selection Criteria

Type	Assessment
Purpose	Estimate threshold heart rate
Intensity	Threshold
Zones	1 (threshold)
% Threshold HR	100%
Mesocycle	Preparation 1 and 2, Competition
Terrain	Flat
Time	75–90 minutes
Heart Zones Points	~175–225

Set(s) by Rider's Fitness Level

	Level 1	Level 2	Level 3	Level 4	Level 5
Number of Repeats	2	2	2	2	2
% Threshold HR	100%	100%	100%	100%	100%
Recovery Interval Time	10 min.	10 min.	10 min.	10 min.	10 min.
Cadence during Effort	90–95 rpm	90–95 rpm	90–95 rpm	90–95 rpm	90–95 rpm

Heart Rate Profile and Rider's Notes

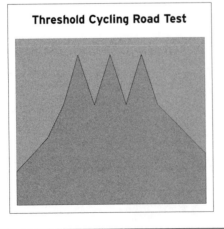

Threshold Cycling Road Test

1. Warm up 20 minutes, including two to three high-intensity, 1–2-minute efforts.
2. Maintain an 8-minute or 3-mile effort at 90–95 rpm at a speed you can barely maintain.
3. Recover 10 minutes. Record time of effort, average heart rate, rate of perceived exertion, and average rpm data.
4. Repeat effort.
5. Record data and warm down 20–30 minutes.

Ride Overview

Choose a relatively flat section of road that is free of stop signs and traffic. The test will last for 8 minutes (or 3 miles) from start to the finish line. You will need a heart rate monitor that calculates average heart rate and either a stopwatch or bike computer with chronograph function. Plan your threshold test when you are fully rested and have not done any hard or high-intensity training for 48 hours.

Warm-up should be about 10–20 minutes at a minimum and include two or three high-intensity efforts of 1–2 minutes each to warm up your legs. Give yourself about 3–5 minutes of easy pedaling between each high-intensity effort. You will want about 10–15 minutes of easy riding prior to the start of the threshold test.

When you are ready, start your heart rate monitor and stopwatch or bike computer. Begin the test by getting up to speed as quickly as possible; then shift into a higher gear and settle into a steady rhythm. Your gearing should allow you to maintain a cadence of 90–95 rpm and a speed that will challenge you to the end. Push yourself to maintain the effort for a total of 8 minutes (or 3 miles) even though it will be uncomfortable. At the end of the effort, record the following information:

- Time of the effort
- Average heart rate
- Rating of perceived exertion

Turn around and ride back to the start. Keep your cadence high and in an easy gear. Repeat the same 8-minute test. When the second test is over, record your data and conclude the ride with 15–30 minutes of easy riding.

To estimate your threshold heart rate take the lower of the two heart rate averages and subtract 3–5 bpm. This will be your threshold heart rate number for cycling until you retest again. We recommend testing every one or two months. When you do retest, make sure you have similar conditions and that you test over the same time or distance.

THRESHOLD ENDURANCE ROAD TEST

Ride Selection Criteria

Type	Assessment
Purpose	Assess threshold and muscular endurance
Intensity	Threshold
Zones	All
% Maximum HR	~80%–90%
% Threshold HR	~100%
Mesocycle	Preparation 1 and 2, Competition
Terrain	Flat
Time	45 minutes–1 hour 40 minutes
Heart Zones Points	~90–175 (maximum and threshold)

Set(s) by Rider's Fitness Level

	Level 1	*Level 2*	*Level 3*	*Level 4*	*Level 5*
Number of Repeats	—	2–3	3–4	4–5	6
% Maximum HR	—	~80%	~85%	~90%	~90%
% Threshold HR	—	~100%	~100%	~100%	~100%
Recovery % Maximum HR	—	60%	60%	60%	60%
Recovery % Threshold HR	—	70%	70%	70%	70%
Work-Recovery Ratio	—	4:1	4:1	4:1	4:1
Cadence for Time Trial	—	90–100 rpm	90–100 rpm	90–100 rpm	90–100 rpm

Heart Rate Profile and **Rider's** Notes

Threshold Endurance Road **Test**

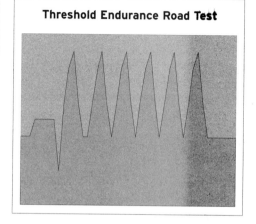

1. Warm up 20–30 minutes in small chainring.
2. Begin 0.5-mile flat course with a rolling start; quickly shift to big chainring and rise out of the saddle building cadence to 90–100 rpm.
3. Shift to a higher gear and hold cadence for the duration of the distance.
4. At end of the 0.5 mile, record your data (average heart rate and elapsed time).
5. Recover heart rate to 60% of maximum or 70% of threshold.
6. Repeat the test up to your fitness level.

Ride Overview

Measure a 0.5-mile flat course. **The goal is to reach** a fast speed and then be able to sustain it for the 0.5 **mile. Begin** with a 20–30-minute warm-up in the small chainring. Start your **bike computer** as you begin the time trial with a rolling start. Shift to the big **chainring** (52/17–19), rise out of the saddle, and quickly build your cadence to **90 rpm;** then shift to a higher gear and hold your cadence for the duration **of the** distance. At the end of the 0.5 mile, record the following:

- Average heart rate
- Elapsed time

Recover your heart rate **to 60 percent** of maximum or 70 percent of threshold. You may also recover **according to** the recommended work interval–recovery time ratio. Repeat the **test to accompany** fitness level, or stop the repeats when two consecutive **elapsed times** go up or you cannot hold 90 rpm.

As you become fitter some or all of the following will happen:

- Your average heart rate drops
- Your elapsed time drops (getting faster)
- Your recovery time between repeats **decreases**
- Your maximum number of repeats increases

All of these are positive training effects that **tell you your training is** working!

APPENDIX B:
HEART ZONES RESOURCES

Branches of the Training Tree for Threshold (T) and Maximum (M) Heart Rate

Branch	Mesocycle	Purpose	Physiological Adaptation	Zone	Terrain
COMPETITION	Competition	Training to reach optimal performance capacity; putting it all together to ride faster and longer	Increased aerobic and nonaerobic capacity; peak readiness	T: z2–5c M: z2–5	Varied
POWER	Prep 2	Improving power while focusing on specific event requirements	Increased aerobic and nonaerobic capacity	T: z2–5c M: z2–5	Varied
STRENGTH	Prep 2	Building volume and intensity with a focus on hills and threshold improvement	Increased aerobic capacity, muscular strength, and endurance	T: z2–5 M: z2–4	Varied
ENDURANCE	Prep 1	Building volume and intensity	Increased aerobic capacity and muscular endurance	z1–3	Flat to hills
BASE	Prep 1	As starting point for training program, gradually building volume or time in the saddle at a low intensity	Aerobic endurance and development of cycling-specific muscles	z1–2	Flat to rolling hills
TRANSITION	Regeneration	A time for regeneration and recovery; goal setting for next season	Physical, mental, and emotional recuperation	z1–2	Cross-training

Five Fitness Levels of Riders

Level 1	Distance	Can ride 5–20 miles at moderate intensity
	Time	Can ride 20–60 minutes without stopping
	Speed	Comfortable speed is under 14 mph
	Experience	Rode less than 3 hours per week in the past year
Level 2	Distance	Can ride 20–50 miles at moderate intensity
	Time	Can ride more than 60 minutes without stopping
	Speed	Comfortable speed is about 14–16 mph
	Experience	Has ridden for more than 1 year and rides more than 3 hours per week
Level 3	Distance	Can ride over 50 miles at a moderate intensity
	Time	Is comfortable with more than 2 hours on a ride
	Speed	Comfortable speed is 16–18 mph
	Experience	Rides about 2,500 miles per year or 300+ miles a month
Level 4	Distance	Enjoys the long rides over 50 miles at a moderate to hard intensity
	Time	Is comfortable with more than 4 hours on some rides
	Speed	Comfortable speed is more than 18 mph
	Experience	Rides about 3,500 to 4,000 miles per year or 400+ miles a month
Level 5	Distance	Enjoys the long rides over 75 miles at a moderate to hard intensity
	Time	Is comfortable with more than 5 hours on some rides
	Speed	Comfortable speed is more than 20 mph
	Experience	Rides about 4,500 to 6,000 miles per year or 500+ miles a month

Heart Zones Ride Selection Criteria

	Type of Ride: Interval (I), Steady State (SS), Combination (C), Recovery (R), Threshold HR Test (TT), Maximum HR Test (MT), or Assessment (A)	Intensity: Aerobic (A), Threshold (T), Nonaerobic (NA), or ATP-PC (ATP)	Mesocycle: Prep 1 (P1), Prep 2 (P2), Competition (C), or Transition (T)	Duration (minutes)	Terrain: Flat (F), Rolling (R), Hills (H), or Varied (V)
RIDES					
Blowout	C	A, T, NA, ATP	P2, C	90–150	F, R
Cadence Drills and Skills	I	A	P1, P2	60–90	F
Comin' Round the Mountain	C	A	P1, P2, C	90–180	F, R, H
Crisscross Zone 2	I	A	P1	60–150	F, R
Crisscross Zone 3	I	A	P1	60–180	F, R
Crisscross Zone 4	I	T, NA	P2, C	60–180	R
Cruisin'	I	T	P2, C	50–90	F
Copy Cat	C	A, T, NA, ATP	P2, C	90–240	V
Easy Rider 1	R	A	P1, T	30–120	F, R
Easy Rider 2	C, R	A	P1, P2, T	30–120	F, R
Easy Rider 3	C, R	A	P1, P2	50–120	F, R
Fix It	C	A	P2, C	60–120	F, R
Galactic	SS	T	P2, C	60–120	F, R
Head for the Hills	I	NA	P2, C	60–90	H
Hiccup	I	NA	P2, C	90–150	H
Holy Smokes	I	A	P2, C	60–90	F, R
Jumpin' Jiminie	C	A, ATP	P2, C	90–150	F, R
Kowabunga	C	A	P2, C	90–150	F, R, H
Pyramid Scheme 1	I	A	P1	60–100	F, R
Pyramid Scheme 2	I	A, T, NA	P2, C	70–100	F, R
Rock Steady	SS	A	P1, P2	60–150	F, R
Sign Here, Press Hard	I	A, NA, ATP	P2, C	60–180	F, R
Silver Streak	C	A, T, NA, ATP	P2, C	60–180	V
Turtle Rock	SS	A	P1, P2, C	75–180	F, R

(continues)

Heart Zones Ride Selection Criteria *(continued)*

	Type of Ride: Interval (I), Steady State (SS), Combination (C), Recovery (R), Threshold HR Test (TT), Maximum HR Test (MT), or Assessment (A)	Intensity: Aerobic (A), Threshold (T), Nonaerobic (NA), or ATP-PC (ATP)	Mesocycle: Prep 1 (P1), Prep 2 (P2), Competition (C), or Transition (T)	Duration (minutes)	Terrain: Flat (F), Rolling (R), Hills (H), or Varied (V)
ASSESSMENTS					
Aerobic Time Trial	A	A	P1, P2, C	45–60	F, R
Cycling Economy Test	A	A	P1, P2, C	60	H
Hill Sprints	MT	NA	P1	45	H
Larger Than Life	MT	NA	P1	45	F
Recovery Interval Ride	A	A, T, NA	P1, P2, C	50–110	F, R
Steady State Ride	A	A	P1, P2, C	30–90	F, R
The All-Out Trip	MT	NA	P1	60	F
Threshold Cycling Road Test	TT	T	P1, P2, C	75–90	F
Threshold Endurance Road Test	A	T	P1, P2, C	45–100	F

Heart Zones Ride-O-Gram

	Aerobic		Threshold	Nonaerobic					ATP-PC		
	Steady State Intervals (longer period of sustained heart rate)			Medium to Long Intervals (>60 sec.)					Short Intervals (<60 sec.)		
	Tempo	Endurance Recovery/Neuro-muscular	Threshold	Hill Sprints	Climbing Acceleration	Non-aerobic Power	VO_2	Race Simulation	Power Starts	PC Jumps	Sprints
Muscular Strength	Turtle Rock	Cadence Drills	Kowabunga	Hill Sprints	Head for the Hills	Holy Smokes	Holy Smokes		Blowout	Blowout	Silver Streak
Kowabunga	Comin' Round the Mountain	Criss-cross Zone 3	Pyramid Scheme 2	Hiccup	Silver Streak	Pyramid Scheme 2	Pyramid Scheme 2	Copy Cat		Jumpin' Jiminie	Pyramid Scheme 2
Comin' Round the Mountain	Criss-cross Zone 3	Criss-cross Zone 4	Cruisin'	Copy Cat		Silver Streak	Copy Cat				Copy Cat
Silver Streak	Rock Steady	Rock Steady	Galactic								
Blowout	Blowout	Easy Rider 1	Silver Streak			Blowout	Blowout				Sign Here, Press Hard
Criss-cross Zone 4	Jumpin' Jiminie	Easy Rider 2	Blowout								Easy Rider 3
Fix It		Easy Rider 3	Criss-cross Zone 4								
		Pyramid Scheme 1									
		Fix It									

Heart Zones Training Tree for Maximum Heart Rate

		Zones				
		1	2	3	4	5
Mesocycle	*Branch*		Aerobic			Non-aerobic
COMPETITION		10%	20%	30%	35%	5%
PREPARATION 2: Event-Specific Training	Power	—	5%	30%	40%	25%
	Strength	10%	10%	30%	50%	—
PREPARATION 1: Conditioning and Technique	Endurance	20%	30%	40%	10%	—
	Base	20%	40%	30%	10%	—
TRANSITION		10%	20%	60%	10%	—

Heart Zones Training Tree for Threshold Heart Rate

		Zones							
		1	2	3	4		5a	5b	5c
Mesocycle	*Branch*		Aerobic			Threshold		Nonaerobic	
COMPETITION		10%	20%	30%	35%	—	3%	1%	1%
PREPARATION 2: Event-Specific Training	Power	—	5%	30%	40%	—	15%	7%	3%
	Strength	10%	10%	30%	50%	—	—	—	—
PREPARATION 1: Conditioning and Technique	Endurance	20%	30%	40%	10%	—	—	—	—
	Base	20%	40%	30%	10%	—	—	—	—
TRANSITION		10%	20%	60%	10%	—	—	—	—

Rides by Training Block

Block 1 PREP 1 Conditioning/Technique	Block 2 PREP 2 Event Specificity	Block 3 COMPETITION Event Training/Racing	Block 4 TRANSITION Regeneration
Cadence Drills	Cadence Drills	Cadence Drills	Easy Rider 1
Crisscross Zone 2	Comin' Round the Mountain	Comin' Round the Mountain	Crisscross Zone 2
Crisscross Zone 3	Pyramid Scheme 2	Pyramid Scheme 2	Pyramid Scheme 1
Rock Steady	Turtle Rock	Turtle Rock	Steady State Ride
Easy Rider 1	Cruisin'	Cruisin'	Easy Rider 2
Easy Rider 2	Easy Rider 2	Easy Rider 2	
Easy Rider 3	Easy Rider 3	Easy Rider 3	
Turtle Rock	Galactic	Galactic	
Pyramid Scheme 1	Head for the Hills	Head for the Hills	
Steady State Ride	Holy Smokes	Holy Smokes	
Fix It	Kowabunga	Kowabunga	
Recovery Interval	Rock Steady	Hiccup	
Comin' Round the Mountain	Copy Cat	Copy Cat	
	Sign Here, Press Hard	Sign Here, Press Hard	
	Silver Streak	Silver Streak	
	Crisscross Zone 4	Crisscross Zone 4	
	Hiccup		
	Fix It		
	Recovery Interval		

Rides by Type

Steady State	Intervals	Combinations	Recovery	Threshold HR Tests	Maximum HR Tests	Assessments
Rock Steady	Pyramid Scheme 1	Kowabunga	Easy Rider 1	Threshold Endurance Test	The All-Out Trip	Cycling Economy Test
Galactic	Cruisin'	Comin' Round the Mountain	Easy Rider 2	Threshold Cycling Test	Hill Sprints	Steady State Ride
Turtle Rock	Head for the Hills	Silver Streak	Easy Rider 3		Larger Than Life	Aerobic Time Trial
	Cadence Drills and Skills	Copy Cat				Recovery Interval
	Holy Smokes	Blowout				
	Crisscross Zone 3	Fix It				
	Crisscross Zone 4	Easy Rider 2				
	Sign Here, Press Hard	Easy Rider 3				
	Hick Up	Jumpin' Jiminie				
	Jumpin' Jiminie					
	Pyramid Scheme 2					
	Crisscross Zone 2					

Ride Protocols According to Energy System

Training Intervals	Aerobic			Threshold	Nonaerobic					ATP-PC		
	Steady State Intervals				Medium to Long Intervals					Short Intervals		
	Muscular Strength	Tempo	Endurance Recovery	Lactate Threshold	Hill Sprints	Climbing Acceleration	Non-aerobic Power	VO_2	Race Simulation	Power Starts	PC Jumps	Sprints
Number of Sets per Ride	2	1	1	1	2	2	2	2	1	2	3	2
Rest between Sets	20 min.	10 min.	N/A	N/A	5 min.	10 min.	15 min.	10 min.	N/A	5 min.	5 min.	15 min.
Number of Repeats	2–5	2	N/A	2–3	3	5	4	3	N/A	3	5	3
Work Interval Time	10 min.	20 min.	N/A	20 min.	30–35 sec.	60 sec.	45 sec.	4 min.	N/A	15 sec.	8–10 sec.	8–15 sec.
Recovery Interval Time	10 min.	10 min.	N/A	5 min.	5 min.	5 min.	5 min.	3 min.	N/A	5 min.	1 min.	5 min.
Work to Recovery Ratio	1:1	2:1	N/A	4:1	1:10	1:5	1:7	4:3	N/A	1:20	1:7	1:20
Cadence During Work Interval	50 rpm	70–75 rpm	80–95 rpm	90–100 rpm	70–80 rpm	80–95 rpm	120 rpm	90–100 rpm	Varies	Build 10 rpm up to 75 rpm	100–130 rpm	135–160 rpm
Heart Rate as % of Maximum Effort	70%–80%	80%	60%–<80%	80%–90%	90+%	90+%	90+%	90+%	Varies	90+%	All-Out	All-Out
Heart Rate as % of Threshold Effort	80%–90%	90%	70%–<90%	90%–100%	105+%	105+%	105+%	105+%	Varies	105+%	All-Out	All-Out

Sample Load Distribution Template for Eight-Month Macrocycle

	Preparation Block			Competition/Event Block				Transition
	8 weeks			20 weeks				4 weeks
	Month 1	Month 2	Month 3	Month 4	Month 5	Month 6	Month 7	Month 8
	=	=	=	=	=	=	=	=
							(event month)	
High								
↑								
Medium								
￨								
Low								

Sample Load Distribution Template for Twelve-Month Macrocycle

	Preparation 1	Preparation 2	Competition	Transition
	Conditioning + Technique	Event-Specific Training	Training to Race	Regeneration
	12 weeks	8 weeks	20 weeks Event Month = Month 10:	8 weeks

Months ⟶	__	__	__	__	__	__	__	__	__	__	__	__
Highest Load												
Higher Load												
High Load												
Medium-High Load												
Medium Load												
Medium-Low Load												
Low Load												
Lower Load												
Lowest Load												

DST

Sport Activity	Distance	Time	Z1	Z2	Z3	Z4	Z5
Date	Distance	Time			Time In Zone		

Summary for the Week	Total Training Time (min):		Z1	Z2	Z3	Z4	Z5
			%	%	%	%	%
Year-to-Date Summary	Total Training Time (min):		Z1	Z2	Z3	Z4	Z5
			%	%	%	%	%

Notes:

Key Workout Type	Averages	am Heart Rate	Body Weight/Fat	Recovery Heart Rate	Weight Training Time	Stretching Time	Training Rating A, B, C, F	HZT Points

AVERAGE OR TOTALS

BPM | LBS. | BPM | MIN. | MIN. | RATING

Notes:

APPENDIX C:
RESTING, DELTA, AND AMBIENT HEART RATES

RESTING HEART RATE

Resting heart rate is usually taken in the morning before you rise from bed. After waking, simply monitor your heart rate before you get up. It is normal for your resting heart to vary within a range of 3–5 bpm in day-to-day readings. Measure your resting heart rate for five consecutive days, and average those measurements for your baseline resting heart rate value. If you notice your resting heart rate exceeding your baseline resting heart rate number by more than 5 bpm, it may be time to focus on recovery. Your heart rate is giving you information about your complex internal physiology. Likely causes for the increase or decrease in heart rate may be your normal and healthy response to stress, dehydration, nutritional changes, overtraining, a poor night's rest, or other events in your life.

There are ranges of resting heart rates. Typically, athletes with high cardiovascular fitness may see resting heart rates of 50–70 bpm, while nonactive people often see resting heart rates of over 60 bpm.

DELTA HEART RATE

This measurement shows the change in heart rate as a result of a change in body position. (*Delta* is the Greek word for "change.") Also known as the *orthostatic test*, delta heart rate is an easy assessment. Lie down in a prone position (P), and relax for about two minutes, noting the lowest heart rate number in this position. At the end of two minutes, stand slowly. Your heart rate may spike briefly and then slowly decrease to a standing heart rate number (S). Note your heart rate after approximately two minutes of standing as it hovers around a standing number.

The formula for finding delta heart rate is

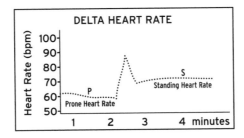

Standing Heart Rate – Prone Heart Position = Delta Heart Rate

Subtract the prone heart rate number (P in the formula) from the standing heart rate (S) to determine your delta heart rate. Typically, the higher your delta heart rate number, the more stressed your body. The lower your heart rate number, the better rested and recovered you may be. The chart here shows a general range of scores for you to compare with your delta heart rate for assessing your training.

Delta Heart Rate	Recommendation
0–10 bpm	Excellent number; your heart is healthy—have a great ride today!
10–20 bpm	Good number; train according to your plan.
20–30 bpm	Train at least one zone lower than you had planned and make it a recovery day.
+ 30 bpm	Take the day off from training.

AMBIENT HEART RATE

Sit and relax for a couple of minutes. Then look at your heart rate monitor. In a sedentary position, your heart is beating at a rate called the *ambient heart rate*.

Your ambient heart rate is a key indicator of both the physical and emotional stresses in your daily life. Your goal is to keep this rate within its normal range. Tracking your ambient heart rate is a wonderful way to use your monitor as a stress monitor.

Your ambient heart rate is affected by internal and external factors: altitude, temperature, some medications, caffeine, and some foods. Feeling tired or achy? Note your ambient heart rate. Is your immune system compromised? Your ambient heart rate may increase 10–15 bpm.

If you notice dramatic changes in your ambient heart rate from what is normal, you should make changes in your training regimen. If it's higher than normal and you were planning a high-intensity workout, consider backing off.

Calculate Your Ambient Heart Rate

Here's a good method for calculating your ambient heart rate.

1 Wear your heart rate monitor throughout your day. When you are in a sedentary position and quiet, observe your heart rate number. This is your ambient heart rate.

2 Over the course of a day, record 6–10 of these ambient heart rate numbers; then average them out at the end of the day.

3 Repeat this process every day for ten days. Has your daily average ambient heart rate changed over the course of the week? How might this relate to your daily stresses? Take notes and reflect, and congratulate yourself for becoming *much* more aware. Remember, the first big step to heart health is awareness.

4 Record your daily average ambient heart rate: _____ bpm

5 Record your average ambient heart rate for the week: _____ bpm

Ambient Heart Rates Ranges (bpm)	
40–60	Excellent
60–70	Very healthy
70–80	Normal
80–90	Indications of emotional, physical, and/ or metabolic stress
90–100	High stress—consider a visit with a medical professional immediately.

INDEX

ABOUT HEART ZONES

THIS IS HEART ZONES™ USA

Heart Zones USA is the world leader in training and education using the heart and the heart rate monitor, metabolic assessments, and DASH© GPS tools. The Heart Zones Training System was created by author and Triathlon Hall of Fame's Sally Edwards and is for anyone who wants to become physically, metabolically, and emotionally fit, healthy, and performing at their best.

Here's a quick overview of our products and services:

- 100+ seminars, workshops, in-service training, certifications, and conferences per year
- Programs and partnerships with health clubs, schools, health organizations, and businesses
- 6 different Do-It-Yourself Kits
- 10 different certifications and over 1,000 certified trainers
- International programs and partners
- Resource-rich website
- Free E-newsletter
- Activity cards for tests and workouts
- Wall charts

- Video DVDs
- Group training programs: Running, Triathlon, Walking, Cycling
- Home study courses
- Personal coaching: Online E-coaching and training
- E-mail training programs: Triathlon and Basic Heart Zones Training
- Zone gear: Jerseys, gear bags, hats, checkout stations, water bottles, shirts

Other Books in the Heart Zones Series

Category	Titles	Author(s)
Training Books	The Heart Rate Monitor Guidebook	Sally Edwards
	The Heart Rate Monitor Log	Sally Edwards
	Heart Zones Training	Sally Edwards
	The Heart Rate Monitor Book	Sally Edwards
	DASH! The Guide to Distance and Speed + Heart Rate	Alinda Perrine and Sally Edwards
Health Books	Heart Zones Health in a Heartbeat	Dan Rudd and Sally Edwards
School Physical Education Books	High School Healthy Hearts in the Zone	Deve Swaim and Sally Edwards
	Middle School Healthy Hearts in the Zone	Deve Swaim and Sally Edwards
Bicycling Books	Heart Zones Cycling	Sally Reed and Sally Edwards
	The Heart Rate Monitor Book for Cyclists	Sally Reed and Sally Edwards
	The Heart Rate Monitor Workbook for Indoor Cyclists	Sally Reed and Sally Edwards
Assessment Books	Heart Zones Testing and Measurement Handbook	Rob Kerr and Sally Edwards
Energy and Weight Management Books	Fit and Fat: An 8-Week Program	Lorraine Brown and Sally Edwards

- DASH! GPS monitors: Distance-Altitude-Speed-Heart Rate monitors
- Professional Resource Zone: Membership for trainers and coaches with tools and support
- Books

Visit us online at www.HeartZones.com

HEART ZONES

Heart Zones USA

2636 Fulton Avenue, Suite 100

Sacramento, California 95821

Phone: (916) 481-7283

Fax: (916) 481-2213

E-mail: staff@heartzones.com

ABOUT THE AUTHORS

Sally Edwards, MS, MBA, has been riding—training and racing—for more than thirty years. In 2001, she was on the winning women's team in Race Across America (RAAM), finishing the 3,100 miles in just seven days. Sally has set world records and won races ranging in length from one mile to the 10-day Eco Challenge adventure race. Starting as a professional runner, Edwards won the Western States 100 Mile Endurance run and capped that by qualifying for the Olympic Marathon trials. She has finished over one hundred Danskin Triathlons, serving for almost 20 years as the national spokeswoman for the Danskin Women's Triathlon Series. She is a successful entrepreneur and founder of Heart Zones USA and Fleet Feet Sports. Currently, Edwards is the CEO and "Head Heart" of Heart Zones USA, an international business that develops educational and training programs using hardware technologies such as heart rate monitors, DASH! GPS tools, power meters, and metabolic meters. She is a popular professional speaker, speaking on such topics as business success, health promotions, motivation, and training to audiences around the world.

Sally Reed, MA, is the athletic director of the prestigious Bellevue Club in Bellevue, Washington, and a competitive endurance cyclist, triathlete, and former USA Cycling Coach. More importantly, in 1997, she created the Heart Zones Cycling training system. After attending one Heart Zones training seminar, she designed, wrote, and started teaching the first Heart Zones Cycling programs that are the basis of this book. For the past eight years, she has traveled around the country coaching athletes, certifying fitness professionals, and teaching seminars, workshops, camps, and programs on Heart Zones Cycling. She has written hundreds of outdoor training rides and indoor workouts for using a heart rate monitor. She is the coauthor of the *Heart Zones Cycling Certification Manual* used by certified coaches and trainers.